The Savvy Client's Guide to Trusts

IS A TRUST RIGHT FOR YOU?

Mary L. Barrow, Esq.

Savvy Client Press

620 Park Avenue, Ste. 242

Rochester, New York 14607

info@savvyclientpress.com

Ordering Information:

Quantity sales. Special discounts are available on quantity purchases by corporations, associations, and others. For details, contact the address above.

The Savvy Client's Guide to Trusts/ Mary L. Barrow. —1st ed.

ISBN 978-0692976159

This book is a brief summary only and should not be used as a substitute for the advice of competent legal counsel from an attorney admitted or authorized to practice law in your jurisdiction. You should always consult your attorney before implementing or changing any estate planning strategy. You should never delay seeking legal advice, disregard legal advice, or commence or discontinue any legal action because of information in this book.

Contents

For Savvy Clients Everywhere

"There's a way to do better...find it."

Thomas Alva Edison

About the Author

Mary L. Barrow has been an attorney for more than 30 years. She has a BA from Brown University and a JD from the University of Pennsylvania law school. For many years she practiced estate planning, probate, and trust law, in three different states, both as a partner in a large law firm and as the principal of a boutique trusts & estates firm. She has helped numerous clients to define their goals and objectives, and then implement those wishes as simply and efficiently as possible through their estate plans.

In 2009 the Osher Lifelong Learning Institute (OLLI) at the University of South Carolina Beaufort asked the author to create a course for its members on the topic of trusts. She was delighted to teach the resulting course for a number of years, and enjoys speaking to groups of non-lawyers on estate planning topics.

She is also the author of *Estate Planning for the Savvy Client: What You Need to Know Before You Meet With Your Lawyer*, the first book in the Savvy Client Series.

Introduction

Welcome to *The Savvy Client's Guide to Trusts*. If you are considering setting up a trust as part of your estate planning, or just want to know more about trusts, then this book is your guide. It is the second book in the Savvy Client Series.

In the first book in the series, *Estate Planning for the Savvy Client: What You Need to Know Before You Meet With Your Lawyer*, I discussed the estate planning process in general, starting with the basics. If you understand the fundamentals, chances are you'll be more confident when meeting with your estate planning lawyer, and you'll make the most of the time, energy, and money you spend on estate planning.

In this book, I'll talk about trusts in more detail and help you consider whether a trust might be right for you. You'll discover what trusts can (and cannot) do, different types of trusts and how they work, and how to weigh the costs and benefits of setting up a trust.

Why I Wrote This Book

I wrote this book because over the years I found that my clients and students had a number of misconceptions about trusts. They had also heard some myths about what trusts can do.

You, too, may have read and heard a lot of things about trusts, and specifically about a type of trust called a "living trust" or "revocable living trust" (which I'll often refer to as an "RLT"). This type of trust is an optional part of your estate plan and is used together with your Will.

Some proponents of RLTs may make blanket statements *without knowing anything about your specific family or asset situation*. You may have heard comments such as:

- "Everyone needs a revocable living trust."
- "You need a revocable living trust to protect your assets."
- "You need a revocable living trust to save on taxes."
- "You need a revocable living trust to avoid probate."

Such statements, of course, invite some questions, such as:

- *Why* does everyone need a revocable living trust?
- Protect my assets *from what*?
- Can a revocable living trust really save on taxes and, if so, *which taxes*?
- What is probate and *why* do I need to avoid it?

On the other side of the coin, some lawyers might shy away from using RLTs, for various reasons, even when an RLT might be appropriate *in your particular situation.*

So which do you think is the correct point of view—pro-RLT or anti-RLT? The answer is *neither.* Whether or not any trust, including an RLT, can help you depends on your goals, where you live, and the specifics of your family and asset situation.

What This Book Is

In this book I'll help you consider whether a trust may be right for you, and I'll dispel some myths and misconceptions about trusts, so that you'll be better informed and more self-confident before you meet with your lawyer. I'll also help you weigh the costs and benefits of setting up a trust.

In **Chapter 1**, I'll ask you a series of questions that will point you to the types of trusts you may want to investigate further, based on your answers to the questions. Then for each type of trust I'll describe the purpose of the trust, how it works (with examples), and in which situations you might want to consider using it. Finally, I'll discuss some truths, myths, and misconceptions about trusts.

Whether you're thinking about establishing a trust, or already have one or more trusts, you'll benefit from reading this book before your next meeting with your attorney. The Savvy Client is you!

What This Book Is Not

This book is not legal advice and it isn't a substitute for legal advice from a qualified attorney experienced in estate planning. It provides a general overview of selected trust concepts in the United States. The book is designed to familiarize you with some basic terms and scenarios—before you meet with your attorney—which might otherwise be confusing to you if you were hearing them for the first time. It is not an all-encompassing guide to trusts.

Keep in mind that specific laws and practices differ in each of the 50 states. Moreover, the information in this book may not apply to your specific situation. You should always consult an experienced estate planning attorney and your tax advisor for legal and tax advice based on your local laws and unique circumstances.

After reading this book, you'll have a greater understanding and be better prepared to work with your lawyer, but you won't be qualified to set up your own trust, plan your own estate, or draft your own estate planning documents any more than you would be qualified to build a car after reading a book on the internal combustion engine. And you won't know more than your attorney (if you suspect you do, get a different attorney).

Finally, reading this book is not intended to and does not create an attorney-client relationship between us, and the book is not a solicitation for legal work.

CHAPTER 1

Should You Have a Trust? Answer These Questions

Your answers to the questions in this chapter will give you a sense of whether you should consider setting up a trust (or more than one) and which type of trust may be right for your situation. If you answer yes to any question, you'll be directed to the type of trust that may interest you. All the trusts are described in the following chapters.

This is a great exercise for you (and your spouse) to do before you meet with your estate planning attorney. It will get you thinking about the types of things that will likely come up during the meeting. If you don't know the answer to a question, it may be a good starting point for a discussion with your attorney.

1. Do you plan to leave assets (money or other property) to minor children or grandchildren? (This means children under the age of 18 or 21, depending on the jurisdiction). If yes, see **Chapter 3, *Trusts for Children.***

2. Are you in a second marriage? If yes, see **Chapter 4, *Trusts for Spouses.***

3. If you are married, are you concerned that after you die your surviving spouse might give or leave assets to a new spouse or "friend"? If yes, see **Chapter 4, *Trusts for Spouses.***

4. If you are married, are you concerned that after you die your surviving spouse may not want to manage assets, may not be capable of managing assets, or may squander assets? If yes, see **Chapter 4, *Trusts for Spouses.***

5. Do you have an adult beneficiary who may not want to manage assets, or may not be capable of managing assets? If yes, see **Chapter 5, *Trusts to Protect a Beneficiary's Inheritance.***

6. Do you have an adult beneficiary who may squander assets? If yes, see **Chapter 5, *Trusts to Protect a Beneficiary's Inheritance.***

7. Do you have a beneficiary who is in an unstable marriage? If yes, see **Chapter 5**, **Trusts to Protect a Beneficiary's Inheritance.**

8. Do you have a beneficiary who may have large outstanding debts? If yes, see **Chapter 5**, *Trusts to Protect a Beneficiary's Inheritance.*

9. Do you have a beneficiary who is in a profession with a high risk of being sued, such as certain medical professions? If yes, see **Chapter 5**, *Trusts to Protect a Beneficiary's Inheritance.*

10. Are you concerned that the assets you leave your beneficiary may be a disincentive to a productive life? If yes, see **Chapter 6**, *Incentive Trusts.*

11. Do you have a beneficiary who, due to illness or disability, currently qualifies for government benefits such as Medicaid or Supplemental Security Income (SSI), or who may qualify for such benefits in the future? If yes, see **Chapter 7**, *Trusts for Those With Special Needs.*

12. Is the value of your gross estate (or if you are married the total of your and your spouse's gross estates combined) close to or more than the federal estate tax exemption? If yes, see **Chapter 8,** *Trusts to Minimize Estate Taxes.*

13. If you live in a state that has an estate tax or an inheritance tax, is the value of your gross estate (or if you are married the total of your and your

spouse's gross estates combined) close to or more than your state's estate tax or inheritance tax exemption? If yes, see **Chapter 8,** *Trusts to Minimize Estate Taxes.*

14. Do you live in a jurisdiction with high probate fees? If yes, see **Chapter 9,** *Revocable Living Trusts to Avoid Probate.*

15. Do you live in a jurisdiction that has a burdensome probate process, for example, requiring confusing paperwork and complicated reports to the court, or that has other difficult or time-consuming requirements? If yes, see **Chapter 9,** *Revocable Living Trusts to Avoid Probate.*

16. Do you live in a jurisdiction where the probate process is slow and may delay the settlement of your estate? If yes, see **Chapter 9,** *Revocable Living Trusts to Avoid Probate.*

17. Do you have hard-to-find heirs? If yes, see **Chapter 9,** *Revocable Living Trusts to Avoid Probate.*

18. Do you have troublesome heirs who might try to challenge your estate plan in court after you die? If yes, see **Chapter 9,** *Revocable Living Trusts to Avoid Probate.*

19. Do you own real estate in a state other than the state of your domicile? If yes, see **Chapter 9,** *Revocable Living Trusts to Avoid Probate.*

20. Do you want to keep your wishes, as expressed in your Will, private? If yes, see **Chapter 9, *Revocable Living Trusts to Avoid Probate.***

21. Do you want to make sure a list of the assets you own at your death does not become public? If yes, see **Chapter 9, *Revocable Living Trusts to Avoid Probate.***

22. Do you want less court involvement in your estate or in any trust you create? If yes, see **Chapter 9, *Revocable Living Trusts to Avoid Probate.***

23. Are you concerned that you may become incapacitated during your lifetime? If yes, see **Chapter 10, *Revocable Living Trusts in Case of Incapacity.***

In the chapters that follow I'll describe some of the most common types of trusts. If you answered yes to any of the questions in this chapter, you'll have a sense of whether a particular type of trust might be useful in your situation. For each type of trust, I'll talk about the purpose of the trust, how it works (with examples), who should consider using it, and whether it can be created as part of a Will (a testamentary trust) or as part of an RLT (a living trust) or both.

The examples will give you a good idea of how these trusts work, help you understand the concepts, and serve as a great starting point for discussion with your attorney, but note that they are not complete illustrations or do-it-yourself directions in any sense. **You should always have an attorney prepare your trust.**

Remember

Answer the questions in this chapter to see if a trust might be useful to you. Your lawyer may have additional suggestions based on your personal situation.

If you don't know the answer to a question, it may be a good starting point for a discussion with your lawyer.

CHAPTER 2

Understanding Trusts

In this chapter, I'll explain some basics about trusts, as well as some important terms and definitions you'll need to know. Mastering this information will not only help you understand the rest of this book, but it will also help you understand your attorney's advice as you discuss trusts with him or her. For readers of *Estate Planning for the Savvy Client*, this chapter will be a good review before we move on to talk about trusts in greater detail.

This book goes beyond the basics of trusts. If you're unclear about the material in this chapter, which is a brief overview of the basics, or have other questions about estate planning, you may want to read *Estate Planning for the Savvy Client*, the first book in the series.

You'll see some words in **bold** print. Those are terms that I'll define in a general, traditional trusts & estates manner.

Bear in mind that each state may have adopted different terms for the same concepts. For example, the person who creates the trust, whom I call the "grantor," is called the "settlor" in some states. This should not interfere with your understanding of the general concepts.

Terms You'll Need to Know

An **estate plan** typically includes:

- a **Will**, also known as a **Last Will and Testament**,
- health care directive(s), known by different names in different states, such as Advance Directive, Living Will, Health Care Power of Attorney, Health Care Proxy and the like, and
- a **power of attorney** for finances.

An estate plan might also include a **revocable living trust** ("**RLT**"), which is an optional part that we'll discuss in detail in **Chapters 9** and **10**.

In estate planning, **property** doesn't just mean real estate; it means *all* of your assets. It includes **real property**, which is real estate, and **personal property**, which is everything else. Personal property includes both **tangible personal property** and **intangible personal property**. Tangible personal property is personal property that you can touch, such as books, jewelry, clothing, furniture and so on. Intangible personal property is personal property that has no physical form, such as bank accounts, stocks, bonds, insurance, annuities, business interests, and the like.

Property = Real Property + Personal Property

Real Property = Real Estate

Personal Property = Tangible Personal Property + Intangible Personal Property

Tangible Personal Property = Property That You Can Touch

Intangible Personal Property = Property That Has no Physical Form

Throughout our discussion of trusts, I will use the terms "property," "assets," and "money" interchangeably to mean anything that you might own.

In estate planning, the deceased person is often called the **decedent** (də-cé-dənt) and, in the case of a married couple, the spouse of a decedent is called the **surviving spouse**.

Your **beneficiaries** are the people you choose to benefit by leaving them property under your Will or through a trust. By contrast, your **legal heirs** are your relatives who have a legal right to inherit your property if you die *without* a Will. In most cases, your legal heirs will be your surviving spouse, your living children, and any children of a deceased child, but this can vary from state to state. If at the time of your death you have no surviving spouse, living children or grandchildren, then the law specifies how your estate will be divided among more remote relatives, such as surviving parents, siblings, nieces, and nephews.

The state that has legal control (**jurisdiction**) over the settlement of your estate generally is the state of your legal residence (**domicile**) when you die. A typical definition of domicile is "a fixed, permanent and principal home to which a person wherever temporarily located always intends to return." You can have more than one residence, but you can have only one domicile. In many cases, it's easy to determine your domicile. However, it can get complicated if you have residences, businesses, or property in more than one state. If you're not sure which state is your domicile, discuss it with your attorney.

Probate is a legal proceeding in which a deceased person's Will is submitted to a court (sometimes called a probate court) that has jurisdiction over the settlement of the deceased person's estate. The court determines whether or not the Will is valid and appoints an **executor** (sometimes called a "**personal representative**") to carry out the terms of the Will. There is usually ongoing court supervision of the progress of the estate administration. Probate requirements, as well as probate fees and expenses, vary enormously not only from state to state, but even from court to court.

Property that passes by Will is typically called **probate property** because a probate proceeding is required to transfer the property to the beneficiaries named in the Will. Property that does not pass by Will, such as property that passes by beneficiary designation and property that passes by law, is typically called **non-probate property**. There does not need to be a probate proceeding to transfer non-probate property. For example, a life insurance company can pay the proceeds of a life insurance policy directly to the beneficiaries of the policy without court involvement. Similarly, some types of jointly-owned property pass automatically by law to the surviving owner without probate.

Many states have a **small estate procedure** designed to handle estates with a value less than a certain amount (typically some number between $25,000 and $150,000). If the probate assets are worth less than the specified amount, then the Will does not have to be probated. Rather, there is a simplified (and usually inexpensive) procedure that allows the probate assets to be distributed in accordance with the Will.

What Exactly Is a Trust?

Broadly speaking, a **trust** is an arrangement by which a person or institution, the **trustee**, legally owns the property of one person, the **grantor**, for the benefit of another person, the **beneficiary**. Here is a common, and simple, example:

> Bonnie, who has a six-year-old son, Alex, is making out her Will. Because it is undesirable to leave a large amount of money to a minor child, the Will includes a trust for Alex. The Will could say something like, "I give and bequeath to my Trustee, Mr. Smith, the sum of X dollars, to be held, administered and disposed of as follows. My Trustee is authorized to pay from time to time so much, or none, of the net income of the trust as may be advisable, in the discretion of my Trustee, for the health, education, maintenance, and support of my son, Alex. When my said son reaches the age of 25 years, my Trustee shall distribute to my said son the entire balance of the trust."

There are generally three parties to a trust:

- The grantor (sometimes also known as the "settlor" or other names) is the person who intends to place property in trust. In our example, Bonnie is the grantor.
- The trustee is the person or institution that legally owns the property for the benefit of another person, and is charged with safeguarding, investing, and distributing the property as directed by the terms of the trust. In our example, Mr. Smith is the trustee.
- The beneficiary is the person who will receive the benefit of the property, but only under the terms of the trust. In our example, Alex is the beneficiary.

A trust divides property ownership into two separate pieces: **legal ownership** and **beneficial ownership**. The trustee is the legal owner of the property in the trust, and the beneficiary is the beneficial owner of the property in the trust.

In our example, Mr. Smith, as trustee, is the legal owner of the property in the trust, but he cannot use the property for his own benefit because he is not the beneficial owner. He can use the property only for the legitimate expenses of the trust and for the benefit of Alex, who is the beneficial owner of the property.

Mr. Smith will be legally obligated to safeguard and invest the trust property until Alex is 25 years old. During that time, Mr. Smith will also decide when and how much of the trust income to spend for Alex's health, education, maintenance, and support. When Alex turns 25 years old, Mr. Smith will pay to Alex whatever property remains in the trust and the trust will end.

More Than One Way to Create a Trust

It's important to understand that there are two common ways to create a trust and the differences between them.

Testamentary Trusts. One way you can create a trust is by including trust language in your Will (as Bonnie did in our example). This is known as a "trust under Will" or **testamentary trust**. Here are some of the characteristics of a testamentary trust:

- A testamentary trust legally exists only after you die and your Will is probated.
- Because the trust doesn't exist until after you die, you can't also be the trustee (as well as the grantor) of your testamentary trust.
- Likewise, because the trust doesn't exist until after you die, you can't fund your testamentary trust during your life. A bit later, I'll explain what it means to "fund" your trust.

Living Trusts. The other way you can create a trust is by using a separate, stand-alone legal document. This is known as an "intervivos" or **living trust**. Here are some of the characteristics of a living trust:

- A living trust is created during your life. It legally exists when you sign the trust document with the necessary legal formalities.
- You can be both the grantor and the trustee of your living trust. The fact that the living trust exists during your lifetime makes this possible.
- You can fund your living trust during your life. That is, you can choose to transfer legal title to property to the trustee. The fact that the living trust exists during your lifetime makes this possible.

Many (but not all) types of trusts can be created either as a testamentary trust or as part of a living trust, so you may have the option of which method to use.

How a Trust Is Created

A trust is usually created in writing by a legal document (the **trust document**). The legal document that creates the trust can be a Will (as in our example), or instead it can be a type of contract between the grantor and the trustee. This type of contract is traditionally called a trust indenture or **trust agreement**, but it may also have other names.

The trust is **created** by a valid trust document, that is, a probated Will or a properly signed trust agreement. The trust document spells out

- the terms and conditions under which the property is to be managed,
- when the trust will end, and

- how the remaining property will be distributed when the trust ends.

How a Trust Is Funded

It is important to distinguish the concept of creating a trust from the concept of funding a trust. Although you may have validly created a trust (by your Will or with a trust agreement), it is not **funded** until you transfer property to the trust. In other words, the trust is funded only when the trustee legally owns some property, known as the **trust property**. (sometimes called the "trust corpus" or other names).

The way you fund a testamentary trust is by leaving property to your trustee in your Will. For example, "I give and bequeath my residuary estate to my Trustee, in trust, to be held, administered, and distributed as follows..." The way you fund a living trust is by transferring property to your trustee, either during your life (for example, by making your trustee the owner of your bank account) or by Will.

What Does a Trustee Do?

The trustee is the person you are "trusting" to safeguard and invest the trust property, pay all the legitimate debts, expenses, and taxes of the trust, and distribute the remaining property in accordance with the terms of the trust document.

A trustee's role can continue for many years, and a trustee may be called upon to exercise **discretion**. This means that if the trust tells the trustee to use the trust property for the "health, maintenance, and support" of a beneficiary, it will be up to the trustee to decide specifically what constitutes the beneficiary's "health, maintenance, and support."

These decisions may be extremely difficult for any number of reasons. For example, let's say the trust was established because the beneficiary is a spendthrift. The beneficiary might demand that the trustee pay for a new sports car or pay off credit card bills. The trustee will need to decide if such expenditures are a prudent use of the trust funds. The trustee may have to consider many factors, such as the size of the trust fund and the beneficiary's other income and resources.

As another example, let's say there is more than one beneficiary of the trust. Should the trustee expend more money on one beneficiary than another? What if one of the beneficiaries needs medical care that, if paid for by the trust, would leave very little for the other beneficiaries? Should the trustee pay for that?

Sometimes these types of questions are answered by the express terms of the trust, but many times they are not. The trustee, therefore, is the one who will need to decide.

"Outright" Versus "In Trust"

Let's say you want to leave a sum of money to someone when you die. Your Will could say something like, "I give and bequeath the sum of X dollars to my son." In this case, when you die, your executor pays X dollars to your son. That X dollars is now the property of your son and he is free to do whatever he wants with it. In this situation you have left the money to your son **outright**.

On the other hand, you could instead leave a sum of money for your son **in trust**. Your Will could say something like, "I give and bequeath the sum of X dollars to my trustee, in trust, for the health, maintenance, and support of my son." In that case, when you die, your executor pays X dollars to the trustee you have named. The money is still for the benefit of your son, but the trustee is the legal owner and must manage it as directed by the trust document until the trust ends. If your son wants to spend the money, he must ask the trustee. The trustee will then decide if what your son wants to spend it on is a good use of the money.

Revocable and Irrevocable Trusts

Certain types of trusts are **revocable** and other types are **irrevocable**. Generally, as the names indicate, you can easily change or revoke a revocable trust, but not an irrevocable trust. Irrevocable trusts usually are not part of a typical estate plan. Be very cautious before transferring assets to an irrevocable trust—it is akin to giving your assets away permanently. If someone suggests that you use an irrevocable trust, make sure it is absolutely necessary. For example, certain types of trusts used for tax minimization must be irrevocable.

For the most part, the types of trusts I'll discuss in this book are revocable trusts; that is, trusts that you can change or get rid of whenever you want during your life (as long as you have sufficient mental capacity).

What Is a Revocable Living Trust?

You may have heard that you need a revocable living trust. Is that true in your case? What exactly is an RLT and why would you need it?

A **revocable living trust** ("RLT") is a trust that you create, not by including trust language in your Will, but rather by signing a stand-alone legal document—a type of contract between the grantor and the trustee. You are the grantor and, because the trust is created while you are still alive, you can also be the trustee.

It's called a "living" trust because it exists while you are still alive (as opposed to a trust under Will, which exists only after you die). It's called a "revocable" trust because you can change or revoke its terms, or even revoke the whole thing, any time you want (as long as you have sufficient mental capacity).

An RLT is an optional part of an estate plan also known as a "Will substitute" because, just like a Will, you can use an

RLT to spell out how you want your assets to pass when you die.

An RLT's most basic functions are to specify

- how the trustee must use the trust property while the grantor is alive,
- who will take over as trustee if the initial trustee (usually the grantor) becomes incapacitated or dies, and
- how the trust property will be distributed when the grantor dies.

Example

Colin signs a trust agreement creating an RLT. The agreement is between Colin, as Grantor, and Colin, as Trustee. The successor Trustee is Colin's son, Earl. The trust agreement says:

- While the Grantor (Colin) is alive, the Trustee (also Colin) shall manage and invest the trust property and pay to the Grantor (himself) whatever amounts of the trust property he wants.

- If the Grantor (Colin) becomes incapacitated, then the successor Trustee (Colin's son, Earl) takes over as trustee, and must use the trust property for the best interests of the Grantor (Colin).

- When the Grantor (Colin) dies, any property remaining in the trust shall be paid to Earl, and the trust ends.

In **Chapters 9** and **10**, we'll discuss some of the uses of RLTs and why you might want one.

Remember

There is more than one way to create a trust.

Don't think that just because you need a trust, you must have a revocable living trust.

Depending on the type of trust you need, you may have the choice of creating it **either** *as part of your Will* **or** *as part of a revocable living trust.*

CHAPTER 3

Trusts for Children

One of the most common types of trusts is a trust to hold assets for the benefit of a minor child—that is, a child under the age of 18 or 21, depending on the jurisdiction. Generally, you can include a trust for children either in your Will or in your RLT (if you have one).

What Is the Purpose?

In many states, a young child cannot directly inherit property valued above a certain (small) amount. For example, as of this writing, the amount in several states is $10,000—the amount may change periodically, but you get the idea. If you leave more than the amount allowed by law, the court will appoint someone to manage and control the assets while the child is a minor. When the child reaches the age of majority (18 or 21), he or she will automatically receive the property outright.

A much better way to provide financially for a child is to set up a trust for him or her. Here are some of the advantages of having a trust:

- You get to appoint the trustee who will manage the property instead of having the court appoint someone after your death.
- The child does not have to receive the property outright as soon as he or she reaches the age of majority. Instead, the trust can continue for as long as you want, even for the child's whole life.
- The trust can specify who will receive the property if the child dies before the trust ends.

How Does It Work?

You include language, either in your Will or your RLT, that says the money or other property you are leaving to the child shall be held in trust for the benefit of the child. When you die, a trustee (whom you name) becomes the legal owner of the property. The trustee must manage the property for the benefit of the child until the trust ends. You also decide when the trust ends, for example, when the child reaches the age you specify or when the child dies.

You have almost complete freedom to specify when the child will receive the trust property. You could say, for example, that the child will receive the trust property outright at the age of 25. On the other hand, you could say that the child will receive half of the trust property at age 25, and the other half at age 40. Or you could say that when the child reaches age 21, he or she will begin receiving all the annual income from the trust property, and then receive the trust property itself at age 62 (or any other age you choose). Or you could choose to say that the property shall be held in trust for the child's whole life; that is, the child will never receive the trust property outright.

Does this mean that while the property is in trust the child receives nothing? No, it does not. Typically, the trust gives the trustee the power to use the trust property for the benefit of the child *in the trustee's discretion.* For example, the trust might say that the trustee can use the property for the "health, education, maintenance, and support" of the child. It will be up to the trustee to decide what expenditures are desirable for the child's health, education, maintenance, and support.

You also have almost complete freedom to specify how the trustee can use the trust property. For example, you could say that the trustee shall pay for the child's wedding or help with the down payment for a first home. However, it's usually best to use general terms that give the trustee the ability to deal with situations that may change over time, like fluctuations in the value of the trust, or medical or other emergencies.

So you see that while the property is in trust it still benefits the child, but the child has to go through the trustee in order to spend money. This can be extremely helpful if, for example, your 18-year-old wants to spend the money on a sports car instead of college. If you don't have a trust, a court-appointed custodian most likely will have to turn over all of the property to the child when he or she reaches the age of majority.

Example #1

Jane wants to leave a bequest to her six-year-old grandson, Timmy. Jane's Will could say something like, "I give and bequeath to my son John, as Trustee, the sum of X dollars, to be held, administered, and disposed of as follows. My Trustee is authorized to pay from time to time so much, or none, of the net income and principal of the trust as may be advisable, in the discretion of my Trustee, for the health, education, maintenance, and support of my grandson, Timmy. When my said grandson reaches the age of 25 years, my Trustee shall distribute to my said grandson the entire balance of the trust."

Example #2

Tom and Janet have three small children, ages 2, 6, and 10. Their Wills could say something like, "If my spouse does not survive me, I give, devise, and bequeath the residue of my estate to my children, in equal shares; provided, however, that if any of my said children has not then reached the age of 25 years, his or her share shall be held by my Trustee, in a separate trust, to be administered and disposed of as follows. My Trustee is authorized to pay from time to time so much, or none, of the net income or principal of such share as may be advisable, in the discretion of my Trustee, for the health, education, maintenance, and support of the beneficiary. When the beneficiary reaches the age of 25 years, my Trustee shall distribute the entire balance of such share to the beneficiary."

Example #3

Helen has an 18-year-old son, Ian, to whom she wants to leave her entire estate. She has an RLT, which could say something like, "After the death of the Grantor [Helen], the Trustee shall pay to the

Grantor's son, Ian, the annual net income of the trust. The Trustee shall also pay from time to time so much, or none, of the principal of the trust as may be advisable, in the discretion of the Trustee, for the health, education, maintenance, and support of Ian. When Ian reaches the age of 25 years, the Trustee shall distribute to Ian one-half the principal of the trust, and when Ian reaches the age of 35 years, the Trustee shall distribute to Ian the entire remaining balance of the trust."

Who Should Consider It?

Anyone who plans to leave a significant amount of money or other property to a minor should consider this type of trust. If you're a young couple just starting out, you may think that you don't have much to leave your children, but don't forget about life insurance. You may (and should) have life insurance, perhaps through your job. Any life insurance proceeds that would otherwise go to your children should be payable to a trust for them instead. Consult with your attorney about how to do this.

Remember

If you're planning to leave a significant amount of money to a minor (such as a minor child or grandchild), always consider leaving it in trust.

Don't forget about life insurance proceeds.

CHAPTER 4

Trusts for Spouses

If you are married, one of the first estate planning decisions you will have to make is whether you wish to leave property to your spouse outright or in trust.

Of course, certain property that you own may pass automatically to your spouse, such as jointly-owned property or other property that passes by law. State law may also give your spouse rights to a portion of your estate (especially if you live in a community property state). We discussed these concepts in greater detail in **Estate Planning for the Savvy Client**. But in this chapter, we're discussing only property that you can legally choose to, and want to, leave to your spouse in your Will or RLT.

You have two main ways of leaving such property to your spouse. The first way is to leave it to your spouse outright. For example, "I give, devise, and bequeath my entire estate to my spouse, if my spouse survives me." This is probably the most common way and is absolutely fine for many couples. But be aware that if you die first and the property passes to your spouse outright, after your death your surviving spouse is free to do whatever he or she wants with the property without restriction. In other words, whichever one of you is the surviving spouse gets to decide who gets your remaining property after both your deaths.

Why might this be a problem in certain situations?

Let's say you're in a second marriage. You have children from a first marriage and your spouse also has children from a first marriage. If you leave everything to each other, then if you die first, your surviving spouse is free not only to spend the money, but also to give it away (perhaps to his or her children, but not yours), or leave it all to his or her children (but perhaps not yours). Upon your spouse's death, your children may get nothing.

Even if you've never been married before, you may be concerned that if you leave property to your spouse outright, and you die first, your surviving spouse may remarry or otherwise become romantically involved with someone and give away or leave the assets to this new person.

Or you may be concerned that if you die first, your surviving spouse may be inexperienced in managing money, or may be ill or elderly or otherwise not capable of managing money.

Rather than leaving property to your spouse outright, you can instead leave it in a **marital trust** (also sometimes called a "QTIP" trust or an "A" trust). Generally, you can include a marital trust either in your Will or in your RLT (if you have one).

What Is the Purpose?

The purpose of a marital trust is to allow you to leave property for the benefit of your surviving spouse during his or her life, while at the same time letting you specify who will receive any property that remains in the trust when your surviving spouse dies. It also allows you to put limits on how the assets can be used during your surviving spouse's life, and to name a trustee other than your spouse, if necessary, to manage the assets.

How Does It Work?

Instead of leaving property outright to your spouse, you include language that says the money or other property that you leave to your spouse shall be held in trust for the benefit of your spouse. When you die, legal ownership of the property passes to a trustee you name. The trustee must manage the property for the benefit of your surviving spouse until the trust ends, usually upon the death of your surviving spouse. At that point, the property passes to the beneficiaries you named in the trust—not to the beneficiaries of your spouse's estate.

In many cases, the trust will specify that the property can be used for the "health, maintenance, and support" of your surviving spouse. You can even name your surviving spouse as his or her own trustee. The goal is to allow your surviving spouse the freedom to use the property as broadly as possible for his or her own well-being, while at the same time preventing him or her from giving the property away or squandering it on something other than health, maintenance, and support, for example, gambling or other vices.

Example #1

Mr. and Mrs. ABC want to leave everything to each other and, after both their deaths, to their two adult children. They each have a Will prepared that says, "I give, devise, and bequeath my entire estate to my spouse, but if my spouse does not survive me, then to my children who survive me, in equal shares." Their attorney points out that whichever one of them dies first is leaving his or her property to the surviving spouse outright. The surviving spouse could conceivably change his or her Will and leave the property to anyone—from a second spouse to a scam artist—and leave nothing to the children. Mr. and Mrs. ABC understand this but are still OK with it based on their personal comfort level.

Example #2

Same example as above, but Mr. and Mrs. ABC are not entirely comfortable and want to protect their children's inheritance in a more tangible way. They each have a Will prepared that says, "I give, devise, and bequeath my entire estate to my Trustee, in trust, for the following uses and purposes. My Trustee is authorized to pay from time to time so much, or none, of the net income and principal of the trust as may be advisable, in the discretion of my Trustee, for the health, maintenance, and support of my spouse during my spouse's life. Upon the death of my spouse, the balance of the trust property remaining shall be paid over and distributed, in equal shares, to my children who are then living. I name my spouse as Trustee of the trust created hereby."

Example #3

Danielle is married to Karl, her second spouse. Danielle has three adult children from a prior marriage. Karl has one adult child from a prior marriage. Danielle wants to leave 70% of her estate to Karl and the other 30% of her estate to her 3 children. If Karl does not survive her, then she wants her entire estate to pass to her three children.

Danielle knows that if she leaves 70% of her estate to Karl outright, and she dies first, then Karl will receive the 70% and her children will receive 30%. But she also knows that when Karl later dies (perhaps as soon as the day after her), that 70% will pass through his estate to his heirs, not hers. Karl will be able to leave it all to his child or to anyone else he wants and Danielle's children could end up with none of it.

So Danielle has her attorney include language that says something like, "If my spouse survives me, I give, devise, and bequeath 70% of my estate to my Trustee, in trust, for the following uses and purposes. My Trustee is authorized to pay from time to time so much, or none, of the net income and principal of the trust as may be advisable, in the discretion of my Trustee, for the health, maintenance, and support of my spouse during my spouse's life. Upon the death of my spouse, the balance of the trust property remaining shall be paid over and distributed, in equal shares, to my children who are then living." She also names someone other than Karl as trustee to minimize direct conflict between Karl and her children over the use of the money.

Example #4

Bob and Barbara have been married for many years. Barbara has always handled the couple's investments, bill paying, and anything else involving finances. Bob has no interest whatsoever in money and does not want to deal with it if Barbara dies first. Barbara leaves her estate to Bob in a marital trust and names

Bob and the couple's trusted accountant as co-trustees.

Example #5

Mr. and Mrs. XYZ want to leave everything to each other, but Mrs. XYZ has a drinking problem. Mr. XYZ is concerned about leaving large amounts of money to Mrs. XYZ if he dies first. Mr. XYZ leaves his estate to Mrs. XYZ in a marital trust and names ABC Bank and Trust as trustee to oversee and manage the money.

Who Should Consider It?

If you are married you may want to consider whether to leave property to your spouse outright or in trust, especially in these situations:

- if you have been married before
- if you want to decide who gets your remaining property after you and your spouse are both deceased—especially if the two of you have different ideas about this
- if you're concerned that your surviving spouse may not be capable of managing assets
- if your surviving spouse does not want to manage assets

Remember

When leaving property to your spouse, consider whether you want to leave it **outright** *or* **in trust.**

CHAPTER 5

Trusts to Protect a Beneficiary's Inheritance

If you leave money or other property to an adult beneficiary outright, then once you die and the property is paid to the beneficiary, it becomes the property of the beneficiary just like any of his or her other property. This means not only that the beneficiary is free to do whatever he or she wants with the property, but that the property may also be vulnerable to the beneficiary's creditors.

You may be reluctant to leave property to a beneficiary who might mismanage or squander it or use it for an undesirable purpose. You also may not want to leave money to a beneficiary if that money will only go to someone else—like a creditor or a divorcing spouse of the beneficiary. After all, it's your money and you don't have to leave it to the beneficiary at all—you could leave it to someone else instead.

But rather than disinherit the beneficiary, is there a way to protect the inheritance?

Yes, leaving property to the beneficiary in trust instead of outright can solve the problem because the trustee you name will have the authority to decide how the money will be managed and spent. The law also typically allows property that you leave in a certain type of trust, sometimes called a **spendthrift trust**, to be protected from your beneficiary's creditors while it is held in trust (that is, while it is legally owned by the trustee—not the beneficiary).

What Is the Purpose?

In general, the purpose of leaving an inheritance to a beneficiary in trust rather than outright is to protect it from the beneficiary's own undesirable actions or from the beneficiary's creditors or potential creditors.

How Does It Work?

You include language that says any property you leave to the beneficiary shall be held in trust for his or her benefit. The trustee you name—who in this case should be someone other than the beneficiary—will have legal ownership of the property and must manage and use the property for the benefit of the beneficiary until the trust ends. You decide for what purposes the property may be used, for example, the "health, maintenance, and support" of the beneficiary. You also decide when the trust will end—which in this case might be when the beneficiary dies—and who receives the balance of the property (if any) when the trust ends.

If protecting the inheritance from the beneficiary's creditors is a concern, you may have to include special provisions in the trust to make it a spendthrift trust. Laws vary from state to state, so check with your attorney about the specific requirements.

Generally, you can include this type of trust either in your Will or in your RLT (if you have one).

Example #1

Fiona helps her elderly father financially from time to time. She wants to be sure that if she dies before her father does, there will be money available for his needs. At this point, she feels that her father is not capable of managing the money himself, so instead of leaving money to him directly, she wants to leave it in trust for him.

Her Will could say something like, "I give and bequeath the sum of X dollars to my Trustee, in trust, for the benefit of my father, for the following uses and purposes. My Trustee is authorized to pay from time to time so much, or none, of the net income and principal of the trust as may be advisable, in the discretion of my Trustee, for the general welfare of my father during my father's life. Upon the death of my father, the balance of the trust property remaining shall be paid over and distributed, in equal shares, to my children who are then living. I nominate and appoint my brother Martin as Trustee of the trust created hereby."

Example #2

Owen and Julia have three adult sons, Tom, Dick, and Harry. Tom and Dick are successful, responsible adults with families of their own. But Harry, although legally an adult, has never held a job, lives in their basement, and plays video games all day. They would like to treat their three sons equally but are concerned about leaving money outright to Harry.

Their Wills could say something like, "If my spouse does not survive me, then I give, devise, and bequeath my entire estate, in equal shares, to my sons who survive me; provided, however that any share for my son Harry shall be held by my Trustee, in a separate trust, for the following uses and purposes. My Trustee is authorized to pay from time to time so much, or none, of the net income and principal of such share as may be advisable, in the discretion of my Trustee, for the health, education, maintenance, and support of my son Harry during his life. Upon the death of my said son, the balance of such share remaining shall be paid over and distributed, in equal shares, to Harry's then living children, if any or, if none, to my then living sons. I nominate and appoint ABC Bank and Trust as Trustee of the trust created hereby."

Example #3

Lisa and Richard have one child, a son, to whom they are leaving their entire estates after they both die. Their son is a mature, responsible adult and there is no reason why he would not be able to handle the money if they were to leave it to him outright. But lately they have noticed some conflict between their son and his wife and have reason to believe that the marriage may go bad. They are concerned that if they leave money to their son outright, it will become part of a divorce settlement and their ex-daughter-in-law might get a hefty chunk of it. So they meet with their lawyer. They change their estate plans to provide that their son's inheritance shall be left to him in a trust that (according to the applicable laws) will help protect the assets from becoming part of a divorce settlement so long as the assets are legally owned by the Trustee and not by their son. They know that once a divorce is finalized, they can always go to their attorney and change things back again so that their son inherits outright.

Example #4

Nicole wants to leave a bequest to her adult granddaughter, but she becomes aware that the granddaughter has a large amount of credit card debt. She is concerned that an outright inheritance will wind up in the hands of creditors. Although Nicole feels strongly that creditors deserve to be paid what is owed them, she has no obligation to pay her granddaughter's creditors. So she meets with her lawyer. They include a trust for her granddaughter that (according to the applicable laws) helps protect the money from creditors and preserves it for other uses that benefit her granddaughter.

Example #5

Same example as above, except that Nicole's granddaughter has no credit card or other debt, but is an ob-gyn—a medical specialist with a high risk of being sued. Nicole is concerned that if her granddaughter receives her inheritance outright, it may become vulnerable to a judgment in a lawsuit. So she meets with her lawyer. They include a trust for Nicole's granddaughter that (according to the applicable laws) helps protect the money from judgment creditors and preserves it for other uses that benefit her granddaughter.

Who Should Consider It?

If at any time you feel that a beneficiary's inheritance should be protected, either from the beneficiary's own actions or from the actions of others, such as in the examples above, you may want to consider leaving the beneficiary his or her inheritance in trust rather than outright. If your beneficiary's creditors are your concern, consult your attorney about the degree of creditor protection available, as applicable laws differ.

Note: Although you may be able to protect a *beneficiary's* inheritance from his or her creditors, typically you cannot protect your assets from *your own* creditors by transferring them to an RLT. An RLT is revocable and, therefore, legally treated the same as property you own outright. (Your state may be an exception—check with your lawyer.) If you're concerned about protecting your own assets from creditors, you might want to consult an attorney experienced in **asset protection law**. There may be certain specialized types of trusts or other techniques that you could explore.

Remember

*If you want to protect the inheritance you leave to a beneficiary from the beneficiary's own actions or the actions of others, consider leaving the inheritance **in trust** instead of **outright.***

CHAPTER 6

Incentive Trusts

Are you concerned that the assets you leave a beneficiary may be a disincentive to that person leading a productive life? Would your beneficiary be tempted simply to live off his or her inheritance and never hold a job? After all, financial necessity is a great motivator. Is it possible that the inheritance could diminish the beneficiary's ambition? Is there anything you can do about it—short of disinheriting the person?

In most of the examples of trusts we have looked at so far, the trustee was directed to use the trust property for the "health, education, maintenance, and support" or the "health, maintenance, and support" of the beneficiary. This is sometimes called the "HEMS" standard. Are these magic words that must be used in a trust? No—you (as the grantor) can direct the trustee to use the trust property in almost any way you choose.

The HEMS standard is commonly used because it is quite broad and allows the trustee the flexibility to make decisions as circumstances change. Also, because it is so commonly used, trustees have a lot of legal guidance when deciding whether a certain expenditure is included in "health, education, maintenance, and support." Therefore, the HEMS standard may be easiest on your trustee.

But that doesn't mean that you have to use that standard. An incentive trust contains instructions to the trustee to make distributions that will (hopefully) influence the beneficiary's behavior in a positive way.

What Is the Purpose?

The purpose of an **incentive trust** is to allow you to give the trustee more specific instructions about when and how to make distributions from the trust to motivate your beneficiary to reach certain goals and achievements, be self-sufficient, and live a productive life.

How Does It Work?

Generally, you can include an incentive trust either in your Will or in your RLT (if you have one). You include instructions to the trustee that are more specific than the HEMS standard. You can place limits on trust distributions in almost any way you wish, keeping in mind how the trust will function as a practical matter. Let's look at some examples.

- You could state that the trustee is only allowed to distribute to the beneficiary, in any given year, an amount no greater than the amount of income earned by the beneficiary from employment. This limitation, of course, will require the trustee to ascertain how much income the beneficiary earns each year from employment.

- You could state that the trustee is only allowed to make distributions for education if the beneficiary is progressing in a course of study that likely will lead to gainful employment. You may want to avoid having a beneficiary who is a perpetual student, but of course the trustee will have to decide what constitutes "progressing" and whether future gainful employment is likely.

- You could direct the trustee to distribute a certain dollar amount to the beneficiary upon graduation from college or completion of the first year of full-time employment. The trustee will have to decide when these requirements are met.

- You could direct the trustee to terminate the trust and distribute the trust assets outright to the beneficiary once he or she has achieved a net worth of a certain amount by his or her own efforts. The trustee will have to obtain the information necessary to determine the beneficiary's net worth.

- You could direct the trustee to use the trust property as a contingency fund that can be used for HEMS only as a last resort. The trustee will have to decide what constitutes a last resort, and will have to obtain the information necessary to make that determination.

- You could limit the trustee to making distributions only if the beneficiary earns a certain dollar amount each year from employment. You may want to provide for an inflation adjustment to that amount. You may also want to make an exception for certain professions (such as teaching or a religious vocation) that are not as financially lucrative. A limitation such as this will require the trustee to make a number of decisions, such as determining how much the beneficiary makes each year from employment, what the inflation adjustment is, and whether the exception applies for a given profession.

Who Should Consider It?

You may want to consider an incentive trust if the amount you're leaving is so large that it may lessen the beneficiary's motivation and you're concerned that the person may underachieve as a consequence.

As we have discussed, the downside to using an incentive trust is that it may be very difficult for the trustee to administer. The trustee may have a hard time determining whether or not a distribution is permitted and how much should be distributed. Situations may change over the life of the trust and after your death you will not be able to change the terms of the trust to conform to the new facts. Your trustee may be able to go to court to change the terms, but that process may be difficult and expensive.

There may be conflicts between the trustee and the beneficiary over these issues. You may not want to burden a family member with such difficult trustee duties, but instead may want to appoint a professional trustee—that is, a bank or trust company. Bear in mind that a professional trustee likely will not consent to act as trustee unless the value of the trust property is above a certain minimum amount.

For all of these reasons, you should discuss with your attorney whether an incentive trust makes sense given the amount you are planning to leave, as well as the other facts of your personal situation.

Remember

You can try to influence a beneficiary's behavior by placing conditions on distributions from an incentive trust.

Keep in mind that this type of trust may be difficult to administer as a practical matter, and may create conflict between the trustee and the beneficiary.

CHAPTER 7

Trusts for Those
With Special Needs

I f you have a beneficiary who, due to illness or disability, currently qualifies for certain government benefits, such as Medicaid or Supplemental Security Income (SSI), or who may qualify for such benefits in the future, it is important to realize that you should not leave property either outright or in a standard type of trust.

Why? A number of government programs, such as Medicaid and SSI, are "**means tested**". In addition to other requirements, they are limited to those people with a financial need. To qualify for benefits, and to continue to qualify for them, a person must have very low levels of both income and resources (assets). Although these qualification levels may change from time to time, they are extremely low. For example, as of this writing, anyone with resources of more than $2,000 ($3,000 for a married couple) is ineligible for SSI. So it's easy to see that an inheritance could jeopardize the benefits of someone who otherwise qualifies for a program.

The good news is that there is a legally sanctioned way for you to leave money to improve a beneficiary's quality of life without disqualifying the person from means-tested benefits. It involves the use of a specific type of trust called a **special needs trust**, or **supplemental needs trust**.

What Is the Purpose?

The purpose of a special needs trust is to supplement the beneficiary's lifestyle without reducing government benefits.

How Does It Work?

The inheritance is placed in a special type of trust. There are strict rules that define how the trustee may use the money. If the trust is set up and administered properly, the assets in the trust will not be counted as income or resources of the beneficiary. For example, the trustee might be able to pay directly for such things as dental care and phone bills, as well as movies, vacations and other types of recreation or entertainment for the beneficiary.

What if you were to use just a typical trust, like the ones we have been discussing, which says that the trustee may use the trust property for the "health, maintenance, and support" of the beneficiary? Generally, that type of typical "support" trust will *not* work as a special needs trust and *would* jeopardize the beneficiary's government benefits because it requires the trustee to support the beneficiary.

Example #1

Mrs. X has four adult children. She doesn't mention to the lawyer who prepares her Will that her daughter Suzy has been receiving SSI and Medicaid for many years. (In fairness to Mrs. X, maybe her lawyer didn't ask.) The Will leaves Mrs. X's entire estate to her children outright, in equal shares. When Mrs. X dies, her other children realize that an outright inheritance will cause Suzy's benefits to stop. This could be catastrophic—private health insurance may not be available. They hire a different attorney, who is able to go to court to establish a special needs trust to hold the money for Suzy and preserve her benefits. This averts disaster, but the whole problem could have been avoided, at much less expense, if the first attorney had known that Suzy should not receive money outright.

Example #2

Same example as above, but because of Suzy's disability, Mrs. X leaves Suzy's share in trust for Suzy's "health, maintenance, and support." This could jeopardize Suzy's benefits in the same way because the trust assets might be "counted" as a resource that is "available" to Suzy. The second attorney is able to go to court to have the trust modified from a support trust to a special needs trust, but again it would have been easier and less expensive to do it before Mrs. X died.

Example #3

Joe and Sharon have a special needs child who may need care into adulthood. They are concerned about what will happen after they both die. They get life insurance on their lives, a good first step. Now they should consult an attorney about the desirability of putting the life insurance proceeds into a special needs trust, which will not disqualify their child from means-tested government benefit programs.

Who Should Consider It?

Anyone who wants to leave money or other property to a beneficiary receiving *means-tested* government benefits, or likely to qualify for such benefits in the future, should consult an attorney experienced with special needs trusts about the best way to do it. Do not leave money or other property to the beneficiary outright and do not leave it to the beneficiary in a standard support trust.

Typically, Social Security, Social Security Disability (SSDI), and Medicare are not means tested. If you are unclear about whether or not a particular program is means tested, consult your attorney.

Caution: Special needs trusts are extremely technical and the law governing them is complex and subject to change. Do not attempt to set up a special needs trust on your own. Consult an attorney who works with these trusts on a regular basis.

What if You Receive Means-Tested Government Benefits?

If you receive means-tested benefits, make sure your family members are aware that they should not leave you money or other property outright or in a standard support trust. If you have a loved one who receives means-tested benefits, make sure other family members (and your attorney) know about the situation. Although it may be possible to correct errors after someone dies, it will probably be difficult and costly. Awareness is the key.

Remember

If you have a beneficiary who qualifies for means-tested government benefits like Medicaid or SSI, do not leave property to him or her outright or in a standard support trust. It could disqualify the person from benefits.

If you qualify for means-tested government benefits like Medicaid or SSI, make sure your family knows that they should not leave you money or other property outright or in a support trust. It could disqualify you from benefits.

CHAPTER 8

Trusts to Minimize Estate Taxes

L et me start off by saying that, for all you may have heard about the estate tax (sometimes called the "death tax") and how bad it is, as a practical matter it affects very, very few people. Why? Because the exemptions from the tax, on both the federal and state levels, are quite high.

Federal Estate Tax

The exemption from **federal estate tax** is $5,490,000 for someone who died in 2017, and was scheduled to increase to $5,600,000 for someone who dies in 2018. The recently passed tax bill roughly doubled the exemptions for the years 2018-2025. As of this writing we don't know the exact amount yet, but for 2018 it could be as much as $11,200,000.

That's right—eleven million, two hundred thousand dollars, and indexed for inflation, so that the exemption amount will rise as inflation rises. Unless the value of your gross estate is more than the exemption amount when you die, your estate is not even required to file a federal estate tax return.

How is the value of your "**gross estate**" determined? Generally speaking, it is the value of everything you own (either individually or jointly with another person) when you die. It includes most anything of value, such as your home, other real estate, financial assets, cash, tangible personal property, retirement plans (such as IRAs and 401(k)s), business interests, life insurance (the death benefit, not just the cash value) and any miscellaneous assets. If you have made certain large gifts during your lifetime, they may also be added in to your gross estate for federal estate tax purposes. Your lawyer can help you figure out what the approximate value of your gross estate (plus lifetime gifts) would be for federal estate tax purposes.

You should consult your lawyer about ways to minimize any potential federal estate tax burden

- if the value of your gross estate, or
- if you are married, the value of your gross estate and your spouse's gross estate combined,

equals more than (or close to) the federal estate tax exemption amount (or you think it might in the future). Irrevocable trusts and other techniques may be able to reduce the federal estate taxes on your estate. As of this writing, the tax rate on amounts above the exemption is a whopping 40 percent.

Caution: Federal estate tax exemption amounts are subject to change. Check with your lawyer.

State Estate and Inheritance Taxes

Most states don't have an estate tax or an inheritance tax. But if you live in a state that does, your estate could be subject to considerable tax because some states have exemption amounts that are lower than the federal exemption amount. As of this writing it appears that the lowest state estate tax exemption amount is $1,000,000 and that maximum state estate tax rates range from 12 percent to 20 percent.

An **estate tax** is based on the value of your entire taxable estate. By contrast, the amount of an **inheritance tax** varies depending upon who is to receive the property. For example, if you leave property to your spouse (and sometimes children), that gift may be exempt from tax. But if you leave property to others, there may be a tax equal to a percentage of that gift.

If your state has an estate tax or an inheritance tax, you should consult your lawyer about ways to minimize the tax burden.

Caution: State estate and inheritance taxes are subject to change. Check with your lawyer.

Credit Shelter Trusts

If you are married, it would be logical to think that if you have an exemption of $11,200,000 and your spouse also has an exemption of $11,200,000, as a couple you could leave up to $22,400,000 worth of property without paying federal estate tax. But before 2011, married couples who left everything to each other lost the benefit of one of their exemptions. (There is a technical tax reason for this, which is not important right now. If you're curious, you can read about it in the Appendix to this book.)

A traditional way to solve this problem was by using **credit shelter trusts** (also known by other names, including "bypass" trusts, "B" trusts, and "family" trusts). Credit shelter trusts are designed to allow married couples to take full advantage of the estate tax exemptions of both spouses.

Effective January 1, 2011 federal law was changed to allow a married couple to take advantage of both of their exemptions (in other words, double the exemption amount) without using credit shelter trusts. A surviving spouse can now use his or her own exemption plus any exemption that was not used by the estate of the first spouse to die. This concept is called **portability**.

What do you have to do to qualify for portability? At the start of this chapter, we learned that unless the value of your gross estate is more than the exemption amount when you die, your estate is not even required to file a federal estate tax return. However, in order to get the benefit of portability, the estate of the first spouse to die must timely file a federal estate tax return, even if a return would not otherwise be required.

If we now have portability, then why am I telling you about credit shelter trusts at all? There are two reasons.

First, if you have an estate plan, you may already have a credit shelter trust. You may have been wondering why you had one. Before 2002, the federal estate tax exemption was a very stable $600,000 (a relatively low amount) for many years. Credit shelter trusts were a standard part of the estate plans of many married couples. Typically these older estate plans required a credit shelter trust to be funded according to a formula.

If you have an older estate plan that makes it mandatory to fund a credit shelter trust, you will want to have it reviewed by your attorney. Not only might that type of plan no longer be necessary, but in some cases it could even cost you more in state estate or inheritance taxes.

Second, even though portability is now available, there are some good reasons why you may still want to have a credit shelter trust as part of your estate plan:

- You may be concerned that portability may not be available to your surviving spouse because your estate has not filed a federal estate tax return—either because your executor was not aware of the requirement or didn't want to incur the expense of filing the tax return.

- You may be concerned that the law will change again—after all, portability was not available before 2011 and may not be in the future.
- If your state has an estate tax, your state's estate tax laws may not allow portability, so a credit shelter trust may still be necessary to fully use both your and your spouse's state estate tax exemptions.
- You can shield all the assets in a credit shelter trust from federal estate tax, even if they increase in value during your surviving spouse's life to more than the original exemption amount. You can't do that with portability—the amount of the unused exemption stays the same over time.

Even if a credit shelter trust is desirable in your case, it has now become important (because of frequent tax law changes) to have maximum flexibility in your plan. You may want to include a credit shelter trust, but leave open the decision of how much to put into the trust until the death of the first spouse. Your lawyer can tell you how to do this.

Caution: Estate tax planning is technical and subject to change. Don't try to do it on your own—always consult your attorney.

Remember

Check the value of your gross estate or, if you are married, your and your spouse's combined gross estates.

Is it greater than the federal estate tax exemption amount?

Do you think it might be in the future?

Do you live or own property in a state that has an estate tax or an inheritance tax?

If you answered yes to any of these questions, consult your lawyer about ways to minimize the tax burden.

Do you have an estate plan that includes a credit shelter trust?

Check with your attorney to see if you still need it. Not only might it no longer be necessary but, depending on where you live, it could even cost you more in state estate or inheritance taxes.

CHAPTER 9

Revocable Living
Trusts
to
Avoid Probate

If you answered "yes" to any of questions 14-22 in **Chapter 1**, you may be interested in avoiding probate. If most of your property is non-probate property, you may already avoid probate (remember that non-probate property doesn't require probate—review **Chapter 2**, *Understanding Trusts*). But if you have a lot of probate property, you can avoid probate by using a revocable living trust (RLT).

Let's review the example of a basic RLT from **Chapter 2**.

Example

Colin signs a trust agreement creating an RLT. The agreement is between Colin, as Grantor, and Colin, as

Trustee. The successor Trustee is Colin's son, Earl. The trust agreement says:

- While the Grantor (Colin) is alive, the Trustee (also Colin) shall manage and invest the trust property and pay to the Grantor (himself) whatever amounts of the trust property he wants.

- If the Grantor (Colin) becomes incapacitated, then the successor Trustee (Colin's son, Earl) takes over as trustee, and must use the trust property for the best interests of the Grantor (Colin).

- When the Grantor (Colin) dies, any property remaining in the trust shall be paid to Earl, and the trust ends.

What Is the Purpose?

Why on earth would anyone enter into a contract with themselves to manage and use their own property?

Although it may seem odd, RLTs have important uses in estate planning. These are two of the most important uses:

- Avoiding probate
- Helping to manage your assets if you become incapacitated.

Your attorney might suggest other reasons why an RLT would be useful in your situation.

In addition, an RLT can contain within it other types of trusts. For example, let's say you want to avoid probate with an RLT, but you also want to set up a marital trust, a credit shelter trust, and a trust for your children. Instead of putting those trusts into your Will, you could instead include them in your RLT.

You can think of an RLT as a container for different types of trusts, much as you can think of an IRA as a container for different types of investments. Putting these trusts in your RLT instead of your Will may help to maintain your privacy and have other advantages, as we will see later in this chapter.

How exactly does an RLT avoid probate? As you have learned, probate is a legal proceeding in which the court determines whether or not your Will is valid. As part of the process, the court also supervises the distribution of your property according to the terms of your Will. But if you have an RLT, the property in it can legally be transferred according to the terms of your RLT. It doesn't pass by Will, and thus no probate is needed. So if you transfer property into your RLT, you can avoid probate.

To avoid probate in this way, you can't simply **create** the RLT by signing a trust document. You have to go a step further and **fund** your RLT during your life. That means you have to transfer ownership of the property to the trustee.

Let's say you have a bank account in your sole name. Ordinarily, when you die there would have to be a probate proceeding (or at least a small estate proceeding) in order to have the bank account transferred to the beneficiary you named in your Will. But if instead of having just a Will you create an RLT (step 1), and then transfer ownership of your bank account to the trustee (step 2), when you die the bank account will be distributed according to the terms of your RLT. It does not pass by Will and, voilà, no probate!

In the example at the beginning of this chapter, we saw that Colin's RLT specified that when he dies, the property in his RLT is to be paid to his son Earl. The trustee will be able legally to distribute the trust property to Earl. Therefore, any property Colin had transferred to his RLT during his life will pass to Earl according to the terms of the RLT without a probate proceeding.

How Does It Work?

Step 1 is to have your attorney prepare a trust agreement which creates the RLT. At a minimum, the agreement should clearly address these items:

- Who is the Grantor (you);
- Who is the initial Trustee (usually also you);
- How the Trustee must use the trust property while the Grantor is alive;
- Who will take over as successor Trustee if the initial Trustee becomes incapacitated or dies; and
- How the trust property will be distributed when the Grantor dies.

Once the trust agreement is signed with the proper legal formalities, the RLT is created.

Step 2 is to fund the RLT with your assets. That means transferring legal ownership of your property to the trustee.

How do you do that? You transfer different types of assets to an RLT in different ways. For example, you typically transfer real estate by signing a new deed; you typically transfer a financial account by changing the ownership of the account with the financial institution; you typically transfer a car at the DMV, and so on.

You Still Need a Will

Even if you have an RLT, you still need to have a Will. Typically, an RLT will be prepared along with a type of Will called a **pourover Will**. A pourover Will simply says that your entire probate estate should be paid over to the trustee of your RLT and distributed in accordance with the terms of your RLT.

For example, a pourover Will might say something like "I give, devise, and bequeath all of my property, both real and personal, to the Trustee under my Revocable Living Trust dated _____, to hold, manage, and control such property under the terms of said trust, and to distribute the proceeds to the beneficiaries therein named according to the terms and conditions of said Revocable Living Trust at the time of my death."

If you are planning to fund your RLT with all of your assets so that at your death you have no probate assets, then why do you need a pourover Will? In short, you still need a pourover Will as a catch-all to handle any unexpected probate assets (for example, assets you forgot to transfer), or assets that cannot be transferred to an RLT (such as a refund that wasn't paid until after your death).

Funding Your Revocable Living Trust

Generally, in order to accomplish the major purposes of an RLT—avoiding probate and/or helping with incapacity—you must complete both step 1 (creating the RLT) and step 2 (funding the RLT by transferring your assets to the trustee).

If it is necessary to fund your RLT in order to accomplish your goals, then you should be as thorough as possible. Understand that you will have to invest time, effort and money to transfer your assets. Make sure you know what the procedure is for transferring each of your assets and whether you will be responsible for getting the assets transferred or whether your attorney's office will be responsible for getting this done.

IRAs and 401(k)s cannot be transferred to an RLT. However, you may remember from reading **Estate Planning for the Savvy Client** that IRAs and 401(k)s pass to the beneficiaries you name on a beneficiary designation form. Because they pass by beneficiary designation, they already avoid probate.

Note: It may be possible to accomplish some estate planning goals by setting up an RLT (step 1) but not funding it (step 2) until the grantor dies (using a pourover Will), and that is the approach taken in some jurisdictions. Check with your attorney.

Do You Lose Control of Your Assets?

But if you transfer legal ownership of your assets to a trustee, doesn't that mean you lose control of them during your lifetime? No—typically you will be both the grantor and the trustee during your life. In addition, your RLT will customarily provide that you can withdraw property from the trust at any time. Finally, your RLT is revocable, so that you can amend or revoke the whole thing at any time (as long as you have sufficient mental capacity).

Because it is *revocable*, it has no effect on your income taxes—that is, you will still file your income tax returns in the same way and all the income from the assets in the RLT will still be included in your personal income.

Also, because it is *revocable*, it has no effect on your federal estate taxes. The trust property will still be included in your federal gross estate for estate tax purposes. If your state has an estate tax or an inheritance tax, chances are it uses the federal gross estate to compute the tax, so you won't save on state estate or inheritance taxes either. (Your state could be an exception—ask your attorney.)

As we discussed in **Chapter 5**, *Trusts to Protect a Beneficiary's Inheritance*, because an RLT is *revocable*, in most cases you cannot protect your assets from your creditors by placing them in an RLT. Assets you transfer to your RLT will be treated the same as property you own outright. (Your state could be an exception—ask your attorney.)

So, generally, if you transfer assets to your RLT, you'll still be able to deal with those assets exactly as you could before. As a practical matter, the only difference will be the name of the legal owner.

Example:

John Doe creates an RLT. The document that creates the RLT says that during John Doe's lifetime, he is both the grantor and the trustee of the RLT. John Doe has a bank account. When John Doe gets his bank statement, it shows that the owner of the account is "John Doe." John Doe contacts his bank and has them transfer the ownership of the account to his RLT. The bank records will then show that the owner is "John Doe, as Trustee of the John Doe Revocable Living Trust dated ____."

John Doe, as trustee, can continue to deal with the account in the same way he did before he transferred it into the RLT. When he files his income tax returns, the income from the assets in the trust will be counted as his personal income, just as if the trust did not exist.

When John Doe dies, any money in the account will be transferred as specified in the RLT, not by Will (and so without probate).

Who Should Consider It?

Whether or not you'll want to avoid probate by using an RLT generally depends on
- where you live; and
- your personal family and asset situation.

Remember that where you live determines which court will have legal authority (jurisdiction) over your estate. Probate procedures (and, therefore, probate costs and other burdens) vary enormously, not only from state to state but also from court to court.

In the rest of this chapter we'll look at some of the factors that might make you want to avoid probate where you live. Your attorney can guide you based on his or her experience with probate in your jurisdiction.

You'll want to weigh the benefits of avoiding probate against the costs in time, effort, and money of not only creating an RLT, but also funding it with your assets. For example, in addition to the legal fees involved in preparing the trust document, there may also be other costs to transfer assets—for example, to have new deeds prepared to transfer your real estate into your RLT.

Probate Fees

Do you live in a jurisdiction with high probate fees? If so, it may be possible for you to avoid probate fees by transferring property to an RLT during your lifetime.

By **probate fees**, I mean the amount required to be paid to the probate court in order to probate a Will and settle an estate. Probate fees are usually set by statute and based on the value of property. There may also be other court fees involved, such as filing fees. In some places the fees are quite reasonable, but in others they are very high and you'll want to avoid them if possible.

In some states the fee is applied only to probate property, so you can avoid probate fees by transferring property to an RLT. But in other states it's impossible to avoid probate fees even with an RLT. If you have an idea of what the probate fees on your estate are likely to be, and if it's possible for you to avoid them by transferring property into an RLT, then you can figure that savings into your cost/benefit analysis.

Example #1

Walter has a probate estate of about $600,000. He is considering transferring his assets into an RLT to save on probate fees. Walter lives in State A, where the probate fees on a $600,000 probate estate are about $750 and the probate process is simple and quick with minimal paperwork. The cost to set up an RLT is about $3,000, with another couple of hundred to transfer his assets. In this case, using an RLT just to save on probate fees and expenses is probably not worthwhile.

Example #2

Same facts, except that Walter has a probate estate of $3,000,000. The probate fees on his estate in State A are about $6,845. In this case it might be worthwhile to avoid these fees by using an RLT.

Example #3

Paula has a probate estate of $10,000,000. She lives in State B, where the probate fees are capped at $1,250 no matter how large the probate estate is. In this case, saving probate fees is not really an issue, but note that there may be many other reasons to use an RLT, especially with an estate of this size.

Legal Fees

Do you live in a jurisdiction where the probate process is burdensome, requiring confusing paperwork and complicated reports to the court, or that has other difficult or time-consuming requirements? If so, you may be able to save on legal fees by avoiding probate.

In some places the probate process is simple, but in others it is expensive and burdensome. The more difficult and complicated the probate process, the more expensive it will be for your estate because there will be more work for your attorney and, therefore, higher **legal fees**.

The probate process is only one part of settling an estate. There will still be other tasks that must be done even if you have an RLT, such as paying taxes and distributing property to the beneficiaries. Your executor (and the trustee of your RLT if you have one) should always hire an attorney to help settle your estate *whether or not you have an RLT*. Why? Because your executor and trustee need to be sure that all legal requirements have been satisfied; otherwise, they could be liable to the beneficiaries.

So while there will always be some legal fees, if your estate can avoid the probate process it may result in less work for the attorney and a lower cost for your estate. Ask your attorney what is involved in the probate process where you live and whether your estate can save on legal fees if you avoid probate. If the probate process where you live is simple and quick, the potential savings from avoiding probate may be negligible. But if the process is complicated and difficult, you could realize substantial savings in legal fees if you avoid it.

Your executor (or trustee) can hire any qualified attorney he or she chooses—it doesn't necessarily have to be the attorney who helped you with your estate plan—and should always discuss fees. Many attorneys charge by the hour, or sometimes a flat fee, for settling an estate.

Note: Don't confuse probate fees, which are paid to the court and set by law, with legal fees, which your executor (or trustee) pays to the attorney and can be any amount they agree upon. Some states have statutory fees that attorneys can charge for settling an estate, but don't be misled into thinking that such fees must be charged. They may simply be the maximum fees that can be charged and your executor or trustee can negotiate a lower fee or an hourly rate instead.

Probate Delays and Roadblocks

Do you live in a jurisdiction where the probate process is slow and may delay the settlement of your estate? If so, you may be able to avoid delays in settling your estate by avoiding probate.

You may have heard that probate is the reason it takes so long to settle an estate. Is that true? It all depends on the probate procedures in the jurisdiction where you live.

In some jurisdictions, the probate process is quick and easy. For example, in some places all the court requires is your original Will, your death certificate, and some simple paperwork, and it will appoint your executor the very same day. But in other places, it could take weeks, if not months, just to have your executor appointed.

This timing is important because your estate needs to have someone with the legal authority to deal with the assets in the estate quickly—for example, to make urgent repairs to real estate, to insure property, or to deal with financial securities that need to be sold right away. A delay could create problems for your estate.

Let's look at one example of the type of probate requirement that can cause delays. If you remember from **Chapter 2**, *Understanding Trusts*, your beneficiaries are the people you choose to benefit by leaving them property under your Will or in an RLT. By contrast, your legal heirs are your relatives who have a legal right to inherit your property if you die without a Will. Probate laws generally require that your legal heirs be given notice of a proceeding to probate your Will. Why? So that they can object to the Will if they think it's not valid.

Some states simply require your heirs to be notified, by regular mail, once your Will has been probated and your executor has been appointed. But beware if you live in a state that requires your legal heirs to be notified before the court will probate your Will and appoint your executor. Such a requirement could delay the appointment of your executor and, in any event, is a bureaucratic burden you may want to avoid. By avoiding probate, you may be able to avoid the legal heir notification requirements.

Hard-to-Find Heirs

Do you have hard-to-find heirs? If so, you may want to avoid probate's legal heir notification requirements.

In the last section, we saw that probate laws generally require that your legal heirs be notified of a proceeding to probate your Will. These requirements can be a big problem if you have hard-to-find heirs. Remember, your legal heirs are not the people you have chosen to benefit in your Will—instead, they are relatives who would inherit your estate if you died without a Will. You may have lost touch with them and not seen or heard from them for many years. For all you know, they could be living in another country, hiking the Appalachian Trail, or even dead.

Of course, they have to be found before they can be notified. In some places, this could delay the appointment of your executor indefinitely. The court might be able to appoint a "temporary" administrator to handle urgent estate matters, but that just adds another layer of bureaucratic expense and delay.

If you live in such a place, you may want to avoid the legal heir notification requirements by avoiding probate.

Will Contests

Do you have troublesome heirs who may try to challenge your estate plan in court after you die? If so, an RLT could be a better way to avoid challenges to your estate plan than simply having a Will.

Some states have probate procedures that may encourage Will contests. For example, you may live in a state that will probate your Will only after your legal heirs sign a paper consenting to the probate or are served with a legal summons. In addition to the expense, delay and potential obstacles, the process may give a troublesome heir false hope that he or she has a right to inherit under your Will. It may even spur the person to contest your Will, which is certainly not desirable.

By avoiding probate, you may be able to eliminate the legal heir notification requirements and other probate procedures that may encourage Will contests. In this and other ways, an RLT could be a useful tool in dealing with troublesome heirs. Your attorney can help you evaluate this option.

Ancillary Probate

Do you own real estate in a state other than your domicile? If so, an RLT could help you avoid having probate proceedings in more than one state.

The state of your domicile (legal residence) is the state that generally has legal authority (jurisdiction) over your estate. However, when it comes to real estate and tangible personal property, it is the state where the property is located—not the state of your domicile—that has jurisdiction over that specific property.

This means that your estate may have to go through two probate proceedings—one in the state of your domicile, and another one in the state where you own real property or tangible personal property. This second probate is typically called an **ancillary probate.**

An RLT can help you avoid an ancillary probate. How? If you transfer your out-of-state property to an RLT, then the property can pass to your beneficiaries according to the terms of the RLT. An ancillary probate typically will not be needed to transfer title to the property. To make sure the title to your out-of-state property is legally transferred to your RLT, you or your attorney should enlist the help of a qualified attorney in the state where the property is located.

Even if you think it's not important to avoid probate in your home state, and are not planning to fund your RLT with your in-state assets, you may still want to transfer title to your out-of-state property to your RLT to avoid an ancillary probate.

Example

Paul lives in State A but has a vacation home in State B. He owns both properties in his sole name. If he dies without an RLT, there will need to be a probate proceeding in State A to transfer his assets according to his Will, and also an ancillary probate in State B to transfer the vacation home. If instead Paul sets up an RLT in his home state and transfers ownership of the vacation home to the trustee of his RLT, then when he dies no ancillary probate will be needed. Ownership of the vacation home will pass according to the terms of the RLT.

Maintaining Privacy

Do you want to keep your wishes, as expressed in your Will, private? Do you want to make sure a list of the assets you own at your death does not become public? If so, you'll be better off using an RLT than simply having a Will.

A probated Will is usually a public document. If you were so inclined, you could walk into many probate courts and read any of the Wills that had been probated there over the years. By contrast, an RLT is not available to the general public and only the trustee and the beneficiaries are likely to know what an RLT says. In some cases, you can even limit a beneficiary's knowledge to only those parts of the RLT that affect him or her.

In what situations might you want to consider keeping your wishes private?

- If you have an unusual or potentially embarrassing family situation. For example, let's say that you have three children. Your Will divides your estate equally among them, but one of your children is bad with money, has a drinking or drug problem, or has marital difficulties, or the like. That child's share is to be held in trust during the child's life. That may not be something you want made public.

- If your Will includes descriptions of assets or bequests to specific individuals or charities. For example, let's say that your cousin, Virginia, is receiving your "sterling silver tea set," or "the sum of fifty thousand dollars." It may be better to keep private the fact that she now owns such valuable property.

- If your Will is very long and complicated and goes on for pages and pages. That's probably a case of "too much information" to reveal in a public document.

Avoiding probate with an RLT can also help you keep information about your assets from becoming public. Traditionally the probate process requires an executor to file with the court a list of all the assets of the deceased (an **inventory**) and an **accounting** that shows exactly what property and how much property each of the beneficiaries received from the estate. In recent years, some courts have revised their procedures in order to protect such sensitive information by, for example, prohibiting account numbers on inventories and accountings. But you may want to go further and prevent these types of documents from having to be filed with the court at all by avoiding probate.

Note: Depending on your state's laws, merely creating the RLT but not funding it until your death may be enough to keep your wishes private. Or you may also need to fund the RLT during your life and avoid probate altogether in order to maintain privacy. Your lawyer can give you more specific information about how the process works in your state.

Less Court Involvement

Do you want less court involvement in your estate or in any trust you create? If so, you can minimize (or even eliminate) court involvement

- in your estate by avoiding probate with an RLT, and
- in any trust you create by setting up the trust in an RLT.

You may feel that the probate process in your state is bureaucratic and intrusive, and is something you would rather avoid. If you use an RLT and avoid probate, you are keeping the court out of your estate.

On the other hand, you may feel that the probate process in your state adds value. For example, you may feel more comfortable having a judge oversee the settlement of your estate and monitor what your executor is doing. In that case, you may feel it is not worthwhile to avoid probate.

The same holds true for any trusts you might create. Remember that in many cases you will have the choice of setting up your trust by creating the trust in your Will (a testamentary trust), or by creating the trust in your RLT.

If you create the trust by Will (a testamentary trust), state law may require the trustee to submit annual reports (accountings) to the court for its approval. This requirement creates an additional expense for the trust and adds a burden of both time and energy on the part of the trustee. On the other hand, if you create the trust in an RLT, normally the trustee is not required to obtain judicial approval of annual accountings (unless the trustee or a beneficiary specifically requests it). If this is the case in your state, you may want to use an RLT to avoid the expense and delay of ongoing court supervision of your trusts.

Of course, if you prefer to have the court monitor the actions of your trustee, then you might be better off with a testamentary trust. Your attorney can help you evaluate your options.

Remember

Use the factors in this chapter to help you decide if you should avoid probate where you live.

If you have mainly non-probate assets, you won't need a revocable living trust to avoid probate because non-probate property already avoids probate.

If you have probate property, you can avoid probate by creating a revocable living trust and funding it with your property.

CHAPTER 10

Revocable Living
Trusts
in
Case of Incapacity

Now let's talk about using a revocable living trust (RLT) to help manage your assets in case you become incapacitated. If you're unclear about what an RLT is, you'll want to review the first part of the prior chapter.

What Is the Purpose?

An essential element of an estate plan is a power of attorney for finances, the purpose of which is to give someone else (your agent) the legal authority to deal with your assets. If you become incapacitated and don't have a power of attorney, a legal guardian may have to be appointed for you through a court proceeding. (If you have questions about powers of attorney or planning in case of incapacity generally, you may want to read *Estate Planning for the Savvy Client*, which discusses the topic in greater detail.)

An RLT is an additional, optional way to plan for incapacity. If you transfer assets into your RLT, and later become incapacitated, a person you name in the RLT (your co-trustee or successor trustee) will have the legal ability to deal with the assets, usually in a more seamless way than if you had only a power of attorney.

How Does It Work?

Typically, you will be the trustee of your RLT during your lifetime. What happens if for some reason you are no longer acting as trustee? For example, you could become incapacitated, die, or just not want to be the trustee anymore.

Co-Trustees. Your RLT could say that you, as well as someone else you name, are **co-trustees**. This means that during your life, both you and your co-trustee are trustees of the trust. If for any reason you stop acting as a trustee, then your co-trustee will have control of any assets in the RLT without a power of attorney. You can name one or more co-trustees. Typically, co-trustees must act unanimously or, if more than two co-trustees, by majority rule.

Successor Trustees. Even if you are the sole trustee during your life, you will name one or more successor trustees in your RLT. A **successor trustee** takes over as trustee if for any reason the initial trustee is no longer acting as trustee. In the example at the beginning of the prior chapter, we saw that Colin's RLT specified that if Colin became incapacitated, then Earl, as successor trustee, would take over managing the assets and using them in Colin's best interests.

What are some of the advantages of using an RLT in addition to a power of attorney? Here are two of them.

First, if you become incapacitated and someone must take over managing your finances, using an RLT could make for a smoother transition. Why?

Banks or other financial institutions may be wary of accepting a power of attorney because it might not be valid or may have been revoked. Although powers of attorney generally have the force of law, as a practical matter a financial institution could refuse to accept a power of attorney, or claim that the bank's own form of power of attorney is the only one it will accept. It may be easier procedurally for the financial institution to accept the authority of a co-trustee, who already has some legal authority over the trust, or a successor trustee named in the trust document, than an agent under a power of attorney.

Second, an RLT lets you define the circumstances under which you will be considered incapacitated. For example, it could say something like "The Grantor shall be considered incapacitated only if so declared by a court of competent jurisdiction or if by reason of illness or mental or physical disability is, in the opinion of two licensed physicians, unable properly to handle the Grantor's own affairs." Or it could say simply that you will be considered incapacitated just because the successor trustee declares you to be so—the determination does not necessarily have to involve physicians. Essentially, you can provide any definition of incapacity you want, tailored to your specific comfort level.

Defining incapacity may not be important to you. After all, you may be like many people, who are comfortable using a general power of attorney. Remember that a general power of attorney takes effect immediately, whether or not you are incapacitated. You don't need to define incapacity because you trust your agent not to use the power unless you do become incapacitated.

Who Should Consider It?

If you are elderly or feel that you may be incapacitated in the near future, and you own assets that can be transferred to an RLT, it may be worthwhile to do so. That way, if you do become incapacitated, the person you name as co-trustee or successor trustee can take over management of the assets.

Let's say you have a number of financial accounts at different banks (or other financial institutions). Without an RLT, your agent will have to give a power of attorney (sometimes an original) to each separate bank to establish himself or herself as your agent on each of the different accounts. This could involve a lot of time and effort, and could delay your agent's ability to manage the accounts. Things might go a lot more smoothly if you consolidated your accounts into one or two banks and transferred the accounts into your RLT.

You Still Need a Power of Attorney

Even if you use an RLT to plan for incapacity, you should still have a power of attorney for finances. Remember that some assets cannot be transferred to an RLT. These include retirement accounts such as IRAs and 401(k)s. You will need to have a power of attorney to allow someone to deal with your retirement accounts and with any other assets outside of the RLT. Make sure your power of attorney gives your agent specific authority to deal with these accounts. You may also want to check with the financial institution in advance.

Example

Christine is a widow who wants her daughter, Mary, to be able to handle banking and bill paying chores for her. Christine makes Mary her agent under a power of attorney.

Christine could also set up an RLT. The RLT document would name herself as the initial trustee and Mary as the successor trustee. The successor trustee would take over as trustee in the event of Christine's death or incapacity. Christine would then transfer ownership of her bank accounts from herself, as an individual, to herself as trustee of the RLT. The bank accounts would become part of the assets of the RLT. If Christine became incapacitated, then Mary, as successor trustee, would be able to control and manage the assets for her mother.

Mary will still need to use the power of attorney if, for example, she needs to withdraw funds from her mother's IRA or 401(k) to pay for her mother's medical expenses.

Revocable Living Trusts and Medicaid

As we saw in **Chapter 7**, *Trusts for Those With Special Needs*, Medicaid is a means-tested government program that, in addition to other requirements, is limited to those individuals with a financial need. In order to qualify for benefits, and to continue to qualify for benefits, a person must have very low levels of both income and assets.

Your RLT will not shelter your assets for purposes of Medicaid planning. Remember that an RLT is *revocable*. Under the Medicaid program, the general rule is that assets you or your spouse place in a *revocable* trust are still considered available resources and count toward the Medicaid income and asset limits.

If qualifying for Medicaid is one of your goals, you should consult an attorney experienced in **elder law** before setting up any trust—whether an RLT or otherwise. Elder law deals with Medicaid, long-term care, nursing home, and other issues of concern to the elderly. While many estate planning attorneys have a working knowledge of how Medicaid operates, not all of them have experience in navigating the complexities of planning for Medicaid eligibility and applying for Medicaid. If you think you may have a need in these areas, you should discuss this with your attorney or prospective attorney.

Remember

A revocable living trust can be helpful if you become incapacitated because it allows a co-trustee or successor trustee to take over the management of assets you have transferred to it.

Some important types of assets, such as IRAs and 401(k)s, can't be transferred to a revocable living trust. You will need a power of attorney to allow your agent to deal with these assets.

Your revocable living trust won't protect your assets for purposes of Medicaid planning. If this is a concern, you should consult an attorney experienced in elder law.

CHAPTER 11

Truth, Myth,
or Misconception?

In this chapter we'll look at some of the things you may have heard about revocable living trusts. For each statement, think about how much of it might be true and whether some or all of it might be a misconception. You can write down your answers in the space provided. Then I'll comment on each statement.

"You Need a Revocable Living Trust to Protect Your Assets"

Can transferring your assets to a revocable living trust protect them? What can it protect them from? Can it protect them from probate fees and expenses? Can it protect them from your creditors? Can it protect them from nursing home expenses?

_____

_____

_____

_____

Comment

If you have an RLT, you can transfer legal ownership of your assets from yourself to the trustee of the RLT (usually yourself). This question asks whether doing that protects your own assets in any way. As we saw in **Chapter 5**, *Trusts to Protect a Beneficiary's Inheritance*, typically you can protect a *beneficiary's* inheritance from the *beneficiary's* creditors by leaving his or her inheritance in a trust (whether RLT or testamentary), but that's not what we're talking about here.

So what can transferring *your* assets to the trustee of your RLT protect them from?

Can it protect your assets from probate fees and expenses?

Depending on where you live, you might be able to save on probate fees and expenses by transferring your assets into a revocable living trust. But remember that is not true in every state, and in some places it may not be worth the expense of setting up and funding the RLT. You may want to review *Probate Fees* and *Legal Fees* in **Chapter 9**.

Can it protect your assets from your creditors?

Transferring your assets to your RLT, *in and of itself*, typically will *not* protect *your* assets from *your own* creditors. Because an RLT is *revocable* (you can withdraw the assets at any time) the assets in the trust are generally considered to be the same as assets owned directly by you. (Your state could be an exception—check with your attorney.) If you're concerned about protecting your own assets from creditors, you may want to consult an attorney who is experienced in **asset protection law**. There may be certain specialized types of trusts or other techniques that you could explore. Don't think that just because you have an RLT, your assets are protected from your creditors.

Can it protect your assets from nursing home expenses?

Transferring your assets to your RLT, *in and of itself*, typically will *not* protect your assets from nursing home expenses. As we saw in **Revocable Living Trusts and Medicaid** in **Chapter 10**, under the Medicaid program, the general rule is that assets you or your spouse place in a revocable trust are still considered available resources and count toward the Medicaid income and asset limits. If qualifying for Medicaid is one of your goals, you should consult an attorney experienced in **elder law** before establishing any trust, including an RLT. Don't think that just because you have an RLT, your assets are protected from nursing home expenses.

"You Need a Revocable Living Trust to Save on Taxes"

Can transferring your assets to a revocable living trust really save on taxes? Which taxes? Can it save on income taxes? Can it save on estate taxes?

_____

_____

_____

_____

_____

Comment

Transferring your assets to your RLT, *in and of itself*, typically will not save on taxes. As we saw in *Do You Lose Control of Your Assets?* in **Chapter 9**, because an RLT is *revocable*, it has no effect on your income taxes—all the income from the assets in the RLT will still be included in your personal income. Also, because the trust is revocable, it has no effect on your federal estate taxes. The trust property will still be included in your federal gross estate for estate tax purposes. If your state has an estate tax or an inheritance tax, chances are it uses the federal gross estate to compute the tax, so you won't save state estate or inheritance taxes either. (Your state could be an exception—ask your attorney.)

However, as you now know, an RLT can be used as a container for other types of trusts. Your RLT could contain within it other trusts designed to save on taxes, such as a credit shelter trust.

It's important to know what the federal estate tax exemption is and, if your state has an estate tax or an inheritance tax, what the exemptions are. If the value of your gross estate (or your and your spouse's gross estates combined) is close to the amounts of those exemptions, you should consult your lawyer about ways to minimize estate taxes. Don't think that just because you have an RLT, you're going to save on taxes.

"You Need a Revocable Living Trust to Avoid Probate"

We have seen that a funded revocable living trust can be used to avoid probate, but why do you need to avoid probate? Are there other ways to avoid probate?

_____

_____

_____

_____

_____

Comment

Before you accept the proposition that you need a revocable living trust to avoid probate, make sure you know why you need to avoid probate. Not everyone needs to avoid probate. As we have seen throughout this book, whether or not you might want to avoid probate depends on where you live and your personal situation. Re-read *Who Should Consider It?* in **Chapter 9, Revocable Living Trusts to Avoid Probate.** Then you can compare the costs and benefits of setting up the RLT as well as funding it.

Also, remember that if you have mostly *non-probate property*, you don't need an RLT to avoid probate because non-probate property *already* avoids probate. Non-probate property is property that does not pass by Will, so no probate is needed. Property that passes by beneficiary designation, such as life insurance, IRAs, 401(k)s, annuities, pensions, and the like, is non-probate property. So is property that passes by law, such as certain types of joint property. We discussed non-probate property in greater detail in **Estate Planning for the Savvy Client.**

"Everyone Needs a Revocable Living Trust"

Throughout this book, we have seen that revocable living trusts are an important element in estate planning and the different things that revocable living trusts can do. Based on what you've learned, do you think that everyone needs a revocable living trust? Why or why not?

_____

_____

_____

_____

_____

Comment

Let's examine this notion based on the two main purposes of an RLT that we have discussed in this book—avoiding probate and helping in case of incapacity. (Note that your attorney might suggest other reasons why an RLT might be useful in your situation.)

Does everyone need an RLT to avoid probate? Not necessarily. As we discussed in the last section, it may not be worthwhile to avoid probate in the jurisdiction where you live. Moreover, you may own mostly non-probate property, which already avoids probate.

Does everyone need to plan in advance in case they become incapacitated? Of course, they do. But does that plan have to include a revocable living trust? Not necessarily. The other, and typically much less expensive, option is to use a power of attorney for finances.

What are the advantages of using an RLT to plan for incapacity? If you have a lot of different financial accounts, it may be easier to transfer them into an RLT, which will give your co-trustee or successor trustee authority over all of them, instead of having your agent go to each financial institution and hope it accepts a power of attorney. As we saw in **Chapter 10**, *Revocable Living Trusts in Case of Incapacity*, it may be easier procedurally for a financial institution to accept the authority of a co-trustee or successor trustee than an agent under a power of attorney. So having an RLT could make the process easier for your agent. An RLT also lets you define the circumstances under which you will be considered incapacitated. That may or may not be important to you.

But don't forget that you'll still need to have a power of attorney for your IRAs, 401(k)s, and any other important assets that can't be transferred to an RLT.

Let's look at some examples of people who pretty clearly don't need a revocable living trust.

Example #1

Carol's major asset is her 401(k) account, which is worth $1,000,000. She also has some small bank accounts—a checking account and a short-term savings account. Does she need an RLT?

At her death, her 401(k) passes to the beneficiary she named on the account's beneficiary designation form—no probate needed. Her small bank accounts can be transferred easily by the small estate procedure in her state, or she can name a beneficiary for those accounts by a making a POD (payable on death) designation with her bank. So Carol doesn't need to avoid probate with an RLT.

If she becomes incapacitated, an RLT won't help with her 401(k)—she must have an agent under a power of attorney for finances to deal with that. Her agent can also deal with the two small bank accounts. So Carol doesn't need an RLT to help with incapacity.

Absent other circumstances, it would be hard to conclude that Carol needs an RLT.

Example #2

Ted has a probate estate of about $600,000, mostly in a brokerage account. He lives in State A, where the probate fees on an estate of that size would be about $750, and the probate process is simple and quick. So avoiding probate is not an issue.

Even if he did want to avoid probate, he could name a beneficiary for his brokerage account by making a TOD (transfer on death) designation with the brokerage.

He owns his (modest) home jointly with his spouse—no probate needed.

If he becomes incapacitated, he has a power of attorney for finances that names his spouse as his agent. If he is concerned that the brokerage firm won't accept the power of attorney when it's needed, he can always check with the brokerage firm in advance to verify what their requirements are.

Again, absent other circumstances, it would be hard to conclude that Ted needs an RLT.

Remember

Generally speaking, transferring your assets to a revocable living trust won't protect them from your creditors, or from nursing home expenses, and it won't save on taxes.

Whether or not you need a revocable living trust to avoid probate depends entirely upon the probate laws and procedures in the state where you live and on your personal family and asset situation.

Your attorney can advise you about probate in your state and suggest options, but make sure they're right for your personal situation.

CHAPTER 12

Choosing a Trustee

In this chapter, I'll discuss some of the duties of a trustee, and the practical considerations you'll want to think about when choosing a trustee. You'll need to consider the purpose of the trust, as well as the personalities of the beneficiaries, in order to find a trustee who's a good fit. The most important consideration is the confidence and trust you have in the trustee you're choosing. You'll want to select a trustee who you think is likely to make distributions from the trust the way you would.

Remember that you can choose to have more than one trustee (co-trustees). If you name co-trustees, it's important that they work well together. Co-trustees must generally act unanimously or, if more than two, by majority rule. If they can't agree, they might need a court to settle disputes, which is something you'll want to avoid.

A Trustee's Duties

A trustee must administer the trust in good faith according to what the trust document says. This means that the trustee must do what the trust tells him or her to do. For example, if the trust says that all the income each year must be paid to the beneficiary, then that's what has to happen, even if the trustee doesn't think the beneficiary should receive the income. On the other hand, if a payment to the beneficiary is not allowed by the trust document, then the trustee can't make the payment no matter how much the beneficiary complains.

We have seen that in some cases the trustee is allowed to use his or her own judgment (discretion), but that can only happen if the trust document clearly allows it by, for example, saying something like, "in the trustee's discretion," or "as the trustee shall determine." As you learned in **What Does a Trustee Do?** in **Chapter 2**, a trustee who has discretion may have to make some difficult decisions.

In addition, a trustee has certain legal duties which are defined by the laws of each state (called **fiduciary duties**). These may vary in some particulars from state to state but, in general, a trustee must usually at the very least:

- act solely in the interests of the beneficiaries (the duty of loyalty),
- treat all beneficiaries fairly if there is more than one (the duty of impartiality),
- administer the trust prudently and only incur costs that are reasonable, and

- invest the trust assets as a prudent investor would (the prudent investor rule).

For example, let's say your trustee decided to use some of the trust money to finance his new business venture. He would be violating a number of his legal duties, and would be liable to the beneficiaries for any damages to the trust.

How are the trustee's duties enforced? Usually a beneficiary or another interested person can ask the court to order the trustee to give a report (sometimes called an **accounting**) of his actions as trustee. If the court finds there has been a violation of his legal duties (sometimes called a **breach of trust**), the court can order a number of remedies, such as requiring the trustee to pay the money back.

Choosing an Individual Trustee

One of your options in naming a trustee is to choose an individual. This could be a family member or friend, or a trusted advisor such as your accountant or attorney. Here are some of the things to consider when naming an individual trustee:

- If you choose a family member or friend, you can decide whether or not they should be paid for acting as trustee and, if so, how much. Although they are usually entitled to a fee, they may be willing to work for free.

- In most cases, a family member or friend will need professional help to administer the trust, such as an attorney to help them with any legal requirements, and a financial advisor to help them invest the trust property prudently. If you have a trusted financial advisor who understands the duties of a trustee, he or she might be able to help your individual trustee.

- Think about the decisions the trustee will have to make, how long the trust will last, and potential conflicts between the trustee and the beneficiaries. Is that a burden you want to put on the person you're considering?

Let's look at some examples.

Example #1

In **Chapter 5,** *Trusts to Protect a Beneficiary's Inheritance* (Example #2), we met Owen and Julia, who have three adult sons, Tom, Dick, and Harry. While Tom and Dick are responsible, Harry is less so, and his share of their estate will be held in trust for his entire life. The trustee of this trust has discretion to use the trust property for the health, education, maintenance, and support of Harry.

Now Owen and Julia have to choose a trustee for Harry's trust. They could name Tom or Dick (or both), but they need to consider the burden that would place on the trustees for a very long time (Harry's whole life), and the potential conflict among the brothers. In this case, they may be better off choosing an unrelated trustee or, if possible, a corporate trustee.

Example #2

In **Chapter 3,** ***Trusts for Children*** (Example #1), we met Jane, who is leaving a bequest in trust for her six-year-old grandson, Timmy. The trust will last until Timmy is 25 years old and, in the meantime, the trustee can use the trust money for the health, education, maintenance, and support of Timmy. Jane named her son, John (Timmy's father), as trustee. In this case, John would be an appropriate choice. After all, as Timmy's father, he already makes decisions about Timmy's health, education, maintenance, and support, and the trust only lasts until Timmy is 25.

Choosing a Corporate Trustee

Another option is to choose a bank or trust company to be the trustee. Not just any bank or financial institution can do this—it must be one that has legal authority to act as a trustee (**trust powers**). Here are some of the things to think about when considering a corporate trustee:

- Corporate trustees will only agree to act as trustee if the value of the trust meets their minimum requirements. For some of the larger institutions, the minimum may be $1,000,000 or more. Some smaller banks or trust companies may have minimums of $500,000 or even less.

- Corporate trustees generally charge for their services based on a fee schedule. The annual fee is usually a percentage of the value of the assets in the trust, for example, one percent of assets under management. This is the same way many financial advisors charge to manage investments. But when considering the costs, remember that a corporate trustee is doing more than just managing money; it is also taking on a trustee's fiduciary duties. You may find that the fees charged by a corporate trustee are no greater than the amount an individual trustee would have to pay for investment management.

- A big advantage of having a professional corporate trustee is its experience in exercising discretion and dealing with beneficiaries, and its expertise in both the investment duties and other fiduciary duties of a trustee.

- If you are considering a corporate trustee, you should meet with several to get an idea of how they operate, what the fees are, and whether you are comfortable with them. For example, some corporate trustees might have local trust officers where you live, but with others you might have to work with someone in another city or state.

- Make sure your trust includes language that allows someone (usually the beneficiaries) to remove the corporate trustee and replace it with a different corporate trustee. This is important in case situations change, such as a merger or changes in corporate personnel.

- You may want your trust to contain language that allows the trustee to terminate the trust and pay the balance to the beneficiaries if, in the trustee's judgment, the value of the trust becomes so small that it's no longer worth the administration expenses (such as trustee's fees) to keep the trust going.

- To get the best of both worlds, you could name a corporate trustee and an individual trustee as co-trustees. The individual trustee would have personal knowledge of the beneficiaries and the family situation, and the corporate trustee would have the expertise to handle the paperwork and other legal requirements.

- What happens if you have a trusted financial advisor who doesn't work for an institution that has trust powers? Let's say your financial advisor works for ABC brokerage, but XYZ trust company will be the trustee of your trusts after you die. Ordinarily, upon your death XYZ trust company would move the money out of ABC brokerage and your financial advisor would no longer be able to manage it. There is a solution to this problem in some states which allow the trustee's duties to be split—the trustee (in this case XYZ trust company) could delegate investment advisory duties to someone else (in this case, ABC brokerage and your financial advisor).

Remember

When choosing a trustee, you'll want to consider:

the purpose of the trust,

how long the trust will last,

the personalities of the beneficiaries,

the confidence and trust you have in the person or institution you choose,

what kinds of decisions the trustee will have to make, and

how much of a burden will be placed on the trustee.

Conclusion

L et's say, hypothetically, you want to hire an architect to design a house for you. You meet with three different architects (A, B, and C). Here is the first thing each of them says to you.

A. "Everyone must have a metal roof."
B. "Let me tell you about flying buttresses."
C. "What kind of house do you want?"

Which architect would you choose? Architect C's question is, of course, the most relevant one. Maybe everyone does need a metal roof, and it might be nice to learn about flying buttresses, but the most important thing is what your goals are.

The same can be said about estate planning. When considering whether you want to use a trust, and what type of trust, these are the questions you should ask:

- What goals am I trying to accomplish?
- Will this technique help me accomplish my goals?
- Is there a simpler and easier way to accomplish the same thing?

I hope this book has given you the confidence to ask these questions and the ability to evaluate the answers. Don't forget—You are the Savvy Client!

Appendix: How Credit Shelter Trusts Work

If you are interested in knowing the technical reasons why credit shelter trusts work, feel free to read this Appendix. If you don't read it, I won't be offended—it's probably a lot more than you want to know.

Credit Shelter Trusts Before 2011

Although it seems logical that if you have a federal estate tax exemption and your spouse has a federal estate tax exemption, as a couple you could leave an estate of up to twice the exemption amount without paying federal estate tax. But before 2011, without proper estate planning, married couples who left everything to each other would lose the benefit of one of their exemptions. Why?

In addition to the estate tax exemption, a married person also receives an unlimited marital deduction. This means that you can leave property to your spouse (or in a qualifying marital trust) in any amount and no federal estate tax will be payable when you die. However, any property that remains at your spouse's death is taxed when your surviving spouse dies.

The unlimited marital deduction does not exempt property from tax; it merely defers the tax until the death of the surviving spouse.

Let's look at some examples. **To make it easier, I'll assume just for purposes of this discussion that the federal estate tax exemption is $5,000,000 (it's not—see Chapter 8,** *Trusts to Minimize Estate Taxes*).

Example #1

Spouse A has a gross estate of $2,000,000 and Spouse B has a gross estate of $1,000,000. Spouse A dies, leaving everything to Spouse B. No federal estate tax is due because of the unlimited marital deduction. Spouse B later dies with a gross estate of $3,000,000— his own estate of $1,000,000 plus the $2,000,000 left to him by his spouse. Spouse B's estate will have to use $3,000,000 of Spouse B's estate tax exemption to eliminate federal estate tax.

To summarize:

- Spouse A dies

- Spouse A's $2,000,000 gross estate passes to Spouse B

- No tax is due because of the marital deduction

- Spouse B later dies

- Spouse B's gross estate is $3,000,000 ($1,000,000 + $2,000,000)

- No tax is due because of Spouse B's $5,000,000 exemption

Example #2

Suppose Spouse A has a gross estate of $4,000,000 and Spouse B has a gross estate of $2,000,000. If Spouse A dies first, leaving everything to Spouse B, there is no estate tax at that point—but not because of Spouse A's $5,000,000 exemption. Rather, there is no tax at that point because of the unlimited marital deduction. Spouse B later dies, leaving an estate of $6,000,000 ($2,000,000 plus $4,000,000). There will be estate tax at Spouse B's death because Spouse B's estate is more than Spouse B's $5,000,000 exemption. So, in effect, Spouse A's exemption was never used and, therefore, was wasted.

To summarize:

- Spouse A dies

- Spouse A's $4,000,000 gross estate passes to Spouse B

- No tax due because of the marital deduction

- Spouse B later dies

- Spouse B's gross estate is $6,000,000 ($2,000,000 + $4,000,000)

- Tax is payable on $1,000,000, which is the amount > Spouse B's $5,000,000 exemption

- Spouse A's exemption is wasted

Couldn't you solve the problem in Example #2 simply by using Spouse A's exemption, instead of the unlimited marital deduction, to exempt Spouse A's $4,000,000 estate? No, because the unlimited marital deduction is *mandatory*. If you leave property to your spouse (or in a qualifying marital trust) your estate must use the unlimited marital deduction.

You can only use the exemption on property that does not qualify for the marital deduction.

One of the traditional solutions to this problem has been to use credit shelter trusts.

What Is the Purpose?

The purpose of a credit shelter trust is to leave property that benefits your spouse but that does not qualify for the unlimited marital deduction. That way, the property in the credit shelter trust can be exempted from tax by your estate tax exemption and will remain free of estate tax forever, no matter what its value is when your surviving spouse dies.

How Does It Work?

A credit shelter trust works by including provisions in the trust that will disqualify it from the unlimited marital deduction. For example, a credit shelter trust will commonly provide that the trust property may be used for the benefit not only of your surviving spouse, but other people as well (such as children or other relatives). Because the trust property does not qualify for the marital deduction, it can instead be exempted by the estate tax exemption.

Example #3

Spouse A has a gross estate of $4,000,000 and Spouse B has a gross estate of $2,000,000. Spouse A leaves his estate to a credit shelter trust that says something like, "I give, devise, and bequeath my estate to my Trustee, in trust, for the following uses and purposes. My Trustee is authorized to pay from time to time so much, or none, of the net income and principal of the trust as may be advisable, in the discretion of my Trustee, to or among my spouse, children, and grandchildren, in such amounts and proportions as may be advisable for their health, maintenance, and support, without regard to equality of distribution."

Because the credit shelter trust allows the trustee to use trust property for the benefit of someone other than the surviving spouse, it does not qualify for the marital deduction.

When Spouse A dies, Spouse A's $5,000,000 estate tax exemption will exempt the $4,000,000 in the credit shelter trust from tax forever. When Spouse B later dies, Spouse B's $5,000,000 exemption can be used to exempt Spouse B's $2,000,000 estate completely—no estate tax at all.

To summarize:

- Spouse A dies

- Spouse A's $4,000,000 gross estate passes to a Credit Shelter Trust

- Spouse A's $5,000,000 exemption exempts the $4,000,000 in the credit shelter trust forever

- Spouse B later dies

- Spouse B's gross estate is $2,000,000

- No tax due because of Spouse B's $5,000,000 exemption

Contrast this result with Example #2 (no credit shelter trust), in which Spouse B's estate had to pay estate tax on $1,000,000 of assets.

Credit Shelter Trusts After 2011

Effective January 1, 2011 federal law was changed to allow a surviving spouse to use any exemption that was not used by the estate of the first spouse to die. The purpose is to permit the couple to take advantage of both of their exemptions (in other words, they can shelter double the exemption amount) without using credit shelter trusts. This concept is called "portability."

Example #4

Same facts as Example #2—Spouse A has a gross estate of $4,000,000 and Spouse B has a gross estate of $2,000,000. If Spouse A dies first, leaving everything to Spouse B, there is no estate tax at that point—but not because of Spouse A's $5,000,000 exemption. Rather, there is no tax at that point because of the unlimited marital deduction. Spouse B later dies, leaving an estate of $6,000,000 ($4,000,000 plus $2,000,000).

But in this example, Spouse A dies after January 1, 2011. Spouse B's estate is able to use both his own $5,000,000 exemption, plus the $5,000,000 exemption that was not used by Spouse A's estate. No tax is due.

To summarize:

- Spouse A dies

- Spouse A's $4,000,000 gross estate passes to Spouse B

- No tax is due because of the marital deduction, no exemption needed

- Spouse B later dies

- Spouse B's gross estate is $6,000,000 ($2,000,000 + $4,000,000)

- No tax is due because Spouse B can use his $5,000,000 exemption plus Spouse A's unused $5,000,000 exemption

Contrast this result with Example #2 (no portability), in which Spouse B's estate had to pay estate tax on $1,000,000 of assets.

In order to get the benefit of portability, the estate of the first spouse to die must timely file a federal estate tax return, even if a return would not otherwise be required. In Example #4 above, in order to obtain portability of Spouse A's exemption, Spouse A's estate must file a federal estate tax return, even though Spouse A's gross estate ($4,000,000) is less than the filing threshold (the exemption amount).

Index

Savvy Client Series

Estate Planning for the Savvy Client:
What You Need to Know Before You Meet With Your Lawyer

The Savvy Client's Guide to Trusts:
Is a Trust Right for You?

Made in the USA
Columbia, SC
03 December 2020

26284840R00074